Intellectual Property Law in Vietnam

Intellectual Property Law in Vietnam

Third Edition

Le Net
Helen Alexandra Morris

This book was originally published as a monograph in the International Encyclopaedia of Laws/Intellectual Property Law.

Founding Editor: Roger Blanpain
General Editor: Frank Hendrickx
Volume Editor: Hendrik Vanhees

Wolters Kluwer

Published by:
Kluwer Law International B.V.
PO Box 316
2400 AH Alphen aan den Rijn
The Netherlands
E-mail: lrs-sales@wolterskluwer.com
Website: www.wolterskluwer.com/en/solutions/kluwerlawinternational

Sold and distributed by:
Wolters Kluwer Legal & Regulatory U.S.
920 Links Avenue
Landisville, PA 17538
United States of America
E-mail: customer.service@wolterskluwer.com

ISBN 978-94-035-1458-1

e-Book: ISBN 978-94-035-1468-0
web-PDF: ISBN 978-94-035-1478-9

The Authors

Qualifications:
PhD (London School of Economics, UK)
LL.M. (Katholieke Universiteit Leuven, Belgium)
LL.B. (Warsaw University, Poland)
Languages:
Vietnamese, English, Polish, French
Memberships:
Ho Chi Minh City Bar Association
Vietnam International Arbitration Centre

Dr Le Net is a Partner of LNT & Partners and has more than twenty-two years of legal practice experience. His practice areas include contract, property and infrastructure, mergers and acquisitions, tax, competition, banking and finance. He has also been active in academia, having taught law at Ho Chi Minh City University of Law, the London School of Economics and the University of the West of England (Bristol). He is also a member of the Vietnam International Arbitration Centre and Singapore International Arbitration Centre. Net has been recommended by many lawyers ranking organizations, including Chambers Global, International Financial Law Review and Legal 500 in the fields of corporate and M&A, banking & finance, infrastructure and property.

Net worked with Baker & McKenzie Ho Chi Minh City since 1998 before becoming a co-founder of LNT & Partners. He has also practised as a foreign lawyer at Baker & McKenzie Brussels and San Francisco and at Clifford Chance Brussels. Together with other members of LNT & Partners, Net has been the lead adviser on many major transactions involving investments, banking/finance, construction and infrastructure. He is in charge of banking/finance and property/infrastructure practice groups in the office. His signature clients are major multinational and large Vietnamese corporations.

Apart from practice, Net has published various works on law in Vietnam and abroad. He is the author of Vietnam's Contract, Corporate Law and Intellectual Property monographs in the International Encyclopaedia of Laws (Kluwer Law International, 1999) – the first English-written academic law book on Vietnam law after the war, and a number of articles published in the *European Competition Law Review*, *World Competition* and *Review of Economic Research on Copyright Issues*. In 2006, Net published three textbooks in Vietnam on Contract Law, Law and Economics and Intellectual Property Law (IPL). In 2009, he edited the *Vietnam – A Foreign Investment Guidebook* of Labour Law Publishing House (written by members of LNT & Partners).

The Authors

Helen Alexandra Morris (born in 1982 in England) is a qualified solicitor of England and Wales and a member of the State Bar of California. She is an experienced senior associate for VCI Legal, Ho Chi Minh City. Previously, she was a senior associate with LNT & Partners, also of Ho Chi Minh City. She is a trainee with Thornleys Solicitors of Manchester, England and seconded to the insolvency team of Hill Dickinson. Helen is a 2003 History and Politics graduate of Salford University, UK. She completed her legal studies at Manchester Metropolitan University, UK, in 2005. Helen has spoken on Vietnamese law on numerous occasions, including at the 22nd Annual LAWASIA Conference and the Irvine Foreign Contractor Tax Seminar. She is the co-author of 'A Guide to Doing Business in Vietnam' and the author of several articles on various aspects of Vietnamese law.

Table of Contents

The Authors 3

List of Abbreviations 13

General Introduction 15

§1. General Background 15
I. Geography 15
II. The Economy 15
III. Political System 16
IV. Social and Cultural Values 17
V. Legal Family 17
VI. The Role of Legislation 18
VII. The Position of Judiciary 19
A. The Courts 19
B. Advocates 19
C. Civil Procedures 20
D. Judge-Made Law 20

§2. Historical Background 21

Part I. Intellectual Property Law 27

Chapter 1. Copyright and Related Rights 27

§1. Sources: Legislation 27

§2. Subject Matter of Protection 27
I. Different Categories of Protected Works 27
A. Works Excluded from Protection 28
B. Special Categories of Works 28
1. Computer Software 28
2. Databases 28
3. Others 29

§3. Conditions of Protection 29
I. Formal Requirements 29
II. Substantive Requirements 30

§4. Ownership 30
I. The Author (Initial Authorship) and the Copyright Holders 30
II. Joint Works/Works Created by Several Persons 31
III. Works Made for Hire 31

§5. Transfer 31
I. Assignment of Copyright 31
II. Licences 32

§6. Scope of Exclusive Rights 32
I. Moral Rights 33
II. Exploitation Rights 33
A. Reproduction Right 33
B. Performing Right 34
C. Adaptation Right (Including Translation Right) 34
D. Other Rights 34
1. Droit De Suite 34
2. Public Lending Right 34

§7. Limitations or Exemptions to the Scope of Copyright Protection 35

§8. Duration of Protection 36

§9. Neighbouring Rights (Related Rights) 36
I. Eligible Subject Matters, Rightholders, Term of Protection 36
II. Scope of Rights 37
A. Rights of Performers and Investors 37
B. Rights of Producers of Audio and Visual Fixation 38
C. Rights of Broadcasters 39
III. Fair Use 40

§10. Infringement and Remedies 40

§11. Overlapping and Relation to Other Intellectual Property Laws 42

Chapter 2. Patents 43

§1. Sources: Legislation 43

§2. Patentable Subject Matter 44

§3. Conditions of Patentability 45
I. Novelty of Inventions 45
II. Inventive Nature of Inventions 45
III. Inventions Which Are Susceptible to Industrial Application 46

§4. Formalities (Procedure for Grant and Obtaining Patent Protection) 46
I. First to File Principle and Priority Date 46
II. General Requirements for Application 46
III. Patent Description, Abstract and Claims 47
IV. Formal Examination 48
V. Publication and Opposition Period 49
VI. Substantive Examination 49
VII. International Application 50
VIII. Refusal to Grant a Patent 50
IX. Grant a Patent 51

§5. Ownership and Transfer (Assignment: Licences) 52
I. Eligible Applicants and Owners 52
II. Assignment of Patents 52
III. Licensing of Patents 53

§6. Rights and Obligations of Patent Owners, the Patent, Entry into National Registry 54
I. Rights of the Patent Owners: Provisional Rights 54
II. Provisional Rights to Inventions 55
III. Obligations to Pay Remuneration to Inventors 55

§7. Limitations and Exceptions to the Scope of Patent Protection: Compulsory Licences 55
I. Prior Use 56
II. Other Limited Uses: Non-commercial Use, Exhaustion of Rights, Use in Transit 56
III. Dependent Invention 57
IV. Public Use 57
V. Grounds for Compulsory Licensing of Inventions 57
VI. Conditions to Grant a Compulsory Licence 58

§8. Duration of Protection: Maintaining and Termination of Patent Protection 59
I. Duration and Termination 59
II. Cancellation of Effectiveness of a Patent 60

§9. Infringement and Remedies 61
I. Acts of Infringement: Rights of Protection 61
II. Remedies to Infringement of Intellectual Property Rights 62
III. Intellectual Property Assessment 62
IV. Civil Action 62
V. Damages 63
VI. Preliminary Injunction (Provisional Urgent Measures) 64
VII. Administrative Penalties 66

§10. Overlapping and Relation to Other Intellectual Property Laws 67

§11. Industrial Property Agents (Patent Agent) 67
I. Rights and Obligations of Industrial Property Agents 67
II. Conditions Applicable to Industrial Property Representation Service Business 68

Chapter 3. Utility Models 70

§1. Sources: Legislation 70

§2. The Protection of Utility Models 72

Chapter 4. Trademarks 73

§1. Sources: Legislation 73

§2. Subject Matter of Protection 74
I. Signs Which May Serve as Trademarks 74
II. Different Categories of Marks 75

§3. Conditions of Protection 76

§4. Formalities (Procedure for Protection, Establishing and Maintaining Trademarks) 78

§5. Ownership and Transfer (Assignment: Licences) 79
I. Right to Register Marks 79
II. Assignment of Trademark 80

§6. Scope of Exclusive Rights 80

§7. Limitations of the Scope of Trademark Protection 81

§8. Use Requirements 81

§9. Duration of Protection: Renewal: Termination 81

§10. Infringement and Remedies 82
I. Definition of Infringements, Measures Against Counterfeit Goods 82
II. Preventive Measures and/or Measures to Secure Enforcement of Administrative Penalties 83
III. Control of Intellectual Property Related Imports and Exports 83
A. Border Control Measures 83
IV. Procedures for Application of the Suspending Customs Procedures 85

§11. Overlapping and Relation to Other Intellectual Property Laws 86

Chapter 5. Trade Names 87

§1. Sources: Legislation 87

§2. The Protection of Trade Names 87

§3. Acts of Unfair Competition 88

Chapter 6. Industrial Designs 89

§1. Sources: Legislation 89

§2. Subject Matter of Protection 90

§3. Conditions of Protection 91
I. Novelty of Industrial Designs 91
II. Creativity of Industrial Designs 91
III. Susceptible of Industrial Application 92

§4. Formalities (Procedure for Grant and Obtaining Protection) 92

§5. Ownership and Transfer (Assignment: Licences) 93

§6. Scope of Exclusive Rights 93

§7. Limitations of the Scope of Protection 93

§8. Duration of Protection 94

§9. Infringement and Remedies 94

§10. Overlapping and Relation to Other Intellectual Property Laws 94

Chapter 7. Plant Variety Protection 95

§1. Sources: Legislation 95

§2. Subject Matter of Protection 95

§3. Conditions of Protection 95
I. Novelty of a Plant Variety 95
II. Distinctness of a Plant Variety 96

III. Uniformity of a Plant Variety 96
IV. Stability of a Plant Variety 96
V. Denominations of Plant Varieties 96

§4. Formalities (Procedure for Grant and Obtaining Protection) 97
I. Method of Filing Applications for Registration of Rights to Plant Varieties 97
II. Priority Principle Applicable to Protection Registration Applications 98
III. Plant Variety Protection Certificates: National Register of Protected Plant Varieties 99
IV. Applications for Registration for Protection 99
V. Formal Examination of Applications for Registration for Protection 100
VI. Substantive Examination 101
VII. Opinions of Third Parties on the Grant of a Plant Variety Protection Certificate 102
VIII. Refusal to Grant a Plant Variety Protection Certificate 102
IX. Suspension and Restoration of Validity of Plant Variety Protection Certificates 103
X. Cancellation of Effectiveness of Plant Variety Protection Certificates 104

§5. Ownership and Transfer (Assignment: Licences) 104
I. Ownership 104
II. Licensing of Plant Varieties 105
III. Assignment of Rights to Plant Varieties 105

§6. Scope of Exclusive Rights 106
I. Rights of Breeders of Plant Varieties 106
II. Extension of Rights of Protection Certificate Holders 106
III. Obligations of Protection Certificate Holders and Breeders of Plant Varieties 107

§7. Limitations of the Scope of Protection: Compulsory Licences 107
I. Limitations on Rights of Plant Variety Protection Certificate Holders 107
II. Compulsory Licensing of Plant Varieties 108
A. Conditions of Compulsory Licensing 108
B. Rights of Protection Certificate Holders in Cases of Compulsory Licensing of Plant Varieties 109

§8. Duration of Protection 109

§9. Infringement and Remedies 109
I. Acts Constituting an Infringement of the Right to a Plant Variety 110
II. Provisional Rights to Plant Varieties 110

§10. Overlapping and Relation to Other Intellectual Property Laws 110

Chapter 8. Chip Protection 111

§1. Sources: Legislation 111

§2. Subject Matter of Protection 111

§3. Conditions of Protection 111
I. Originality of Layout Designs 111
II. Commercial Novelty of Layout Designs 112

§4. Formalities (Procedure for Grant and Obtaining Protection) 112

§5. Ownership and Transfer (Assignment: Licences) 112

§6. Scope of Exclusive Rights 113

§7. Limitations of the Scope of Protection 114

§8. Duration of Protection 114

§9. Infringement and Remedies 114

§10. Overlapping and Relation to Other Intellectual Property Laws 114

Chapter 9. Trade Secrets/Confidential Information 115

§1. Sources: Legislation 115

§2. The Protection of Trade Secrets/Confidential Information 115

§3. Ownership, Scope of Protection and Transfer 115

§4. Obligation to Protect Test Data 117

Chapter 10. Geographical Indications and Appellations of Origin 118

§1. Sources: Legislation 118

§2. Subject Matters of Protection 118

§3. Conditions of Protection 118

§4. Formalities of Protection 119

§5. Ownership, Early Termination and Transfer 120

§6. Infringements and Remedies 121

Selected Bibliography 123

Index 125

List of Abbreviations

IPL	Intellectual Property Law
NOC	National Office of Copyright
NOIP	National Office of Intellectual Property
PCT	Patent Cooperation Treaty
TRIPS	Trade Related Aspects of Intellectual Properties
WIPO	World Intellectual Property Organization
WTO	World Trade Organization

List of Abbreviations

General Introduction

§1. General Background

I. Geography

1. Vietnam is located in the South East Asian region and covers an area of over 330,362 square kilometres. Its shape is similar to a long letter S. The country is surrounded on the eastern and southern sides by the East Sea (Pacific) and the Thailand Gulf, on the northern side by China and on the western side by Laos and Cambodia. Apart from the mainland, some islands near Vietnamese shores (*inter alia*, Phu Quoc and Con Dao) and the two archipelagos, Paracells (Hoang Sa) and Spratlys (Truong Sa) also belong to Vietnam. Vietnam is subdivided into sixty-three provinces and cities, including two metropoles: Hanoi and Ho Chi Minh City.

2. Vietnam's history dates back to at least 2,500 years. Its name 'Vietnam' (South of Viet country) refers to the position of a country in the south of Viet (in Chinese 'Yueh'), an ancient Chinese kingdom. According to some other concepts, 'Vietnam' means 'land of the southern Viet people', but proof of such meaning has never been clear. The official language is the Vietnamese language, which is spoken by the Viet people. Though a large part of the Vietnamese vocabulary is borrowed from Chinese, it was written in a Latin script, invented by Alexandre de Rhodes in the seventeenth century and elaborated on in the early twentieth century. Furthermore, there are several dialects among the people in the northern, central and southern areas.

The currency is the Dong, and the State's status is a socialist republic, dating from 2 September 1945, the date President Ho Chi Minh proclaimed independence. The capital of Vietnam is Hanoi in the North, but the largest city and industrial hub is Ho Chi Minh City (formerly known as Saigon) in the South. The population amounts to about 100 million inhabitants, and it is one of the most densely populated countries in Asia. More than 60% of the population still lives in rural areas where the agricultural economy is dominant.

II. The Economy

3. Vietnam is a developing country, with a Gross Domestic Product (GDP) per capita of approximately USD 4,162 in 2022. Since 1986, thanks to the Doi Moi (reformation) policy and the increase in foreign investment, Vietnam ranks among the countries with the highest economic growth rates in the region and it is one of the largest rice exporters. However, the country's export products are mainly garments, rice and raw materials, such as oil and coal. Vietnamese goods have a low contribution of intellectual property rights. The ratio of Vietnamese patents to total patents submitted or registered at Vietnam's patent office – the National Office of Intellectual Properties (NOIPs) – is among the lowest in the region.

III. Political System

4. Vietnam is a socialist country. The current Constitution (2013) consists of 120 articles divided into eleven chapters which follow a preamble embodying the policy and legislation of Doi Moi. As to the economic system, it is stated that:

> The Vietnamese economy is a socialist-oriented market economy with varied forms of ownership and economic sectors; the state economy plays the dominant role. (Constitution, Art. 51).

Under the current Constitution, freedom of enterprise is also recognized. However, individual rights and freedoms must yield to collective interests. Hence, freedoms may be restricted from time to time by the law when it appears to be contrary to the Constitution's purposes.

While the economy is a 'multi-component commodity', politics are under the leadership of a single party: the communist party of Vietnam (the 'Party'). The Party is a large organization which has many para-administrative organs, expanding down to the lowest administrative levels, under the leadership of a General Secretary. He is elected by the Party's National Congress which is held once every five years.

5. The National Assembly is the supreme legislative body and consists of 499 deputies. It consists of only one Chamber with a term of five years. Any citizen over 18 years of age may vote, and those over 21 may stand for election. Candidates are normally introduced by the Party, the Government and the Fatherland Front. According to statistics from the most recent election, about 26% of deputies are women. Recently, there has been a trend to give more powers to the General Assembly and start a process called democratization at the local administrative level (villages and wards).

The Assembly elects the Prime Minister who will nominate his ministers to establish the Government, subject to the approval of the National Assembly. The Assembly also elects the President of the State Council (the 'President'). The President together with the Prime Minister and the General Secretary of the Party form a triumvirate of powers in Vietnam. In short, Vietnam is a State of laws, with a division of powers along legislative, executive and judicial lines. The State is constructed under a principle of 'concentrated democracy' under the leadership of the Communist Party.

IV. Social and Cultural Values

6. Like in all Far Eastern countries, Vietnamese culture has been shaped by Buddhism, Confucianism and Taoism. Confucianism is based on fundamental individual obligations toward collective structures, Taoism favours the state of resignation, flexibility and modesty, and Buddhism views life as a 'circle between reason and consequence'. Hierarchy, trust and loyalty are cornerstones of harmony.

Vietnamese cultural values are now mixed with various foreign influences, the most visible of which come from China and France. For example, the tradition of codification in Vietnamese law is inherited from the French culture, but the reluctance to bring a dispute into court is most probably derived from Taoism, a philosophy from China.

V. Legal Family

7. While features of the French legal family are still visible in Vietnamese contract law today, it would be a mistake to think that the current Vietnamese Civil Code is only patterned after the French Napoleonic Code. Laws of other socialist and ex-socialist countries, such as Russia and China, have also strongly influenced Vietnamese civil law. With the long history of wars, foreign influences and its specific political system, it is difficult to classify the Vietnamese legal system as part of any legal family. For certain, the Vietnamese legal system is a civil law legal system.

8. In the feudal periods, Vietnamese monarchies focused on building a strong and disciplined State to protect the country from aggression from abroad rather than on establishing a civil society. Criminal law was severely imposed, while civil relationships were flexibly governed. Therefore, Vietnamese law is difficult to fit, in a Western way of categorization, into any particular 'legal family'. Civil relations were governed by a basically criminal code, the Hong Duc Code (or Quoc Trieu Hinh Luat), adopted by King Le Thanh Tong in 1483. However, even at that time, Vietnamese civil law was relatively developed with regard to property law and procedural law (*see* paragraphs 34 et seq. *infra*). Civil wars and the stagnation of the economy in the sixteenth century resulted in the decline of feudalism. People also worried little about their economic rights.

9. During the eighty-year colonial period, starting from 1865, the French imposed the Napoleonic Code on Indochina, including Vietnam. The French legal tradition continued in the South until 1975. Imposing French law on Vietnam did not mean that the people knew French law by heart, nor that the courts at that time followed the principles of liberté, egalité et fraternité of the Napoleonic Code. Dating back to the 1930s, many Vietnamese jurists claimed that French law at that time was just an instrument of French colonizers against the indigenous Vietnamese.[1]

1. Vuong Quang Nhuong (thèse doctorat 1930), *Des conflicts de lois en Indochine*, Paris, 148–152.

During the period of real-socialism (1954–1986), the idea of private property was not encouraged and as such the raison d'etre of the Civil Code disappeared. The old judiciary system was abolished. New judges did not know French law; thus, as time passed by, the influence of French law in Vietnam waned. Instead, the law on obligations is mostly influenced by the Civil Codes of socialist countries, most notably the Principles of Civil Law of the People's Republic of China, the Civil Codes of the Russian Federation, the Soviet Republic and the former German Democratic Republic. Vietnamese theorists worry little about the identity of Vietnamese law. They will adapt any laws, with appropriate modification, as long as they are suitable to the socio-economic situation of the country.

VI. The Role of Legislation

10. Departing from the classical doctrine of the separation of powers, legislative power is exercised by the Government and National Assembly together.

11. In Vietnam, law is not simply a body of rules enacted by the National Assembly. The National Assembly meets in only two sessions a year, each session lasting for fifteen days. Therefore, only the most important acts are passed as laws: the codes, budget and various tax laws, and some important economic laws such as foreign investment law or credit institution law.

The remaining part of Vietnamese law is regulated by ordinances from the Standing Committee President and the sub-law documents, such as decrees, circulars, decisions and directives. The National Assembly passes laws, the Standing Committee issues ordinances, and the Government issues decrees. Those laws and sub-laws are subject to further interpretation and are sometimes supplemented by circulars, resolutions and decisions from the Ministries explaining the application of the higher legislation. Decrees are sometimes issued with attached Regulations. To date, there is no Constitutional court, as in other democratic countries, to exercise a judicial review of decrees and regulations. Such control is in the hands of the National Assembly, assisted by the State investigation agency.

12. The primacy of legislation is not yet the prevailing characteristic of the Vietnamese legal system; many executive organs also exercise legislative functions. This is because of the philosophy behind the concept of law. According to Marxist philosophy, law is not a rationale developing into written documents but an expression of the will of the ruling class, an instrument of the ruling class and serving the interests of the ruling class, who represent the majority of the society (the working class). Without understanding this philosophy, it may not be easy to understand why Vietnamese law is so special and is differently regulated with regard to certain issues, such as State monopolies in some economic sectors, approvals, requirements in contract enforcement over land or different kinds of properties.

VII. The Position of Judiciary

A. The Courts

13. The judiciary consists of independent judges who are selected by the President. The organization of the judiciary is provided in the Law on People's Judicature. There are three levels of ordinary courts in Vietnam (the 'People's Courts'). These are the District People's Courts, Provincial or City People's Courts and the People's Supreme Court. Apart from ordinary courts, there are also special tribunals such as administrative courts, economic courts and labour courts which form part of the Provincial People's Court, and military tribunals. The People's Supreme Court supervises and directs the judicial activities of People's courts, military tribunals and special tribunals.

District courts deal, generally speaking, with less important criminal and civil cases, whereas the more important cases together with labour cases and economic cases are dealt with by the People's Provincial Courts. Appeals against rulings by the district courts may be lodged with the provincial courts. There are also courts of appeal affiliated with the People's Supreme Court in Hanoi, Ho Chi Minh City and Da Nang. Finally, there is a possibility of cassation by the People's Supreme Court. The cassation does not re-assess the facts of a case but only reviews the legality of the rulings from a procedural or material viewpoint.

Administrative disputes are dealt with by either the supervisory administrative organs or administrative courts. To date, examples of the activities of administrative courts remain limited.

14. The Ministry of Justice is responsible for the management of local courts. In principle, Judges are elected, are independent and obey the law only. Cases are also decided by People's laymen together with judges. A person elected as a judge or a People's layperson must be a Vietnamese citizen who is loyal to the Fatherland and socialism and has both the required legal knowledge and a determined spirit to protect the socialist legal system. There is still no specific legal education required for judges in Vietnam. Some of them have not finished university legal education but instead have considerable experience.

B. Advocates

15. There is, in principle, only one lawyer's profession in Vietnam, that of 'luat su' (advocate). Advocates are admitted to the Bar after being sponsored by a senior advocate (one senior advocate can sponsor only one junior advocate during the latter's training period) and will be voted on and admitted to the Bar as a junior advocate. Afterwards, junior advocates must follow a training period typically lasting two years. Advocates must not be public officers or work for foreign law firms. The rule of sponsorship has substantially strengthened the possibility of law graduates being admitted as advocates.

However, it is not compulsory to use advocates in court. It is also not compulsory for the defender of the parties before the courts to be an advocate. With leave of the court and a power of attorney from the plaintiff/defendant, any person may perform the role of advocate before the court.

C. *Civil Procedures*

16. Every case of the first instance is tried and decided by a trial council, normally consisting of one judge and two People's laymen. People's laymen have the same voting power as judges in deliberation. A court decision is rendered on a majority vote.

17. Civil procedures and economic procedures are subject to the Civil Procedural Code 2015. A case is to be presented and argued orally at the public hearing before the court. In principle, the parties have the same rights and obligations and are encouraged to discontinue or compromise actions and determine the issues which come up for adjudication. The parties have the right to be defended by lawyers or other so-called People's defenders.

A provincial court consists of a civil court, criminal court, labour court, economic court and administrative courts. Administrative courts may be involved in civil cases, such as compensation for damage in tort caused by civil servants. Criminal courts may also hear civil cases and render decisions on compensation for an injured person. Apart from that, there is a possibility of criminalization of civil cases, as discussed in paragraph 20 below. Civil courts do not hear disputes arising out of 'economic contracts'. Such disputes are settled by the economic courts. For the difference between civil contracts and economic contracts, *see* paragraph 22 *infra*.

D. *Judge-Made Law*

18. In the past, as in most civil law countries, judges in Vietnam only apply law and do not make law. However, court decisions do have a persuasive influence, especially before the adoption of the Civil Code. During that time, the People's Supreme Court periodically issued 'Reports from Trial Works' (báo cáo xét xử). The purpose of such Reports is to fill the gaps that have yet to be dealt with by the Civil Code. These reports have, therefore, created precedents for lower courts to follow. Recently, the Supreme Court of Vietnam has issued several precedents. Precedents issued by the Supreme Court of Vietnam are not the entire judgments or decisions that have taken legal effect; instead, selected portions of judgments or decisions are chosen to be developed into precedents. Precedents may only select specific arguments or rulings related to a particular content within the judgment or decision chosen for development into a precedent. However, the sole source of Vietnam's legal system remains statutory laws (legal normative documents). Precedents are not a source of law; therefore, they are only applicable to legal situations where there is no legal source to resolve or, even if there is a legal source, there is a difference in interpretation, and in practice, a legally effective court decision has been made to address a similar legal situation.

However, Judges in Vietnam are reluctant to be creative. Sometimes, they even refuse to apply a provision which has already been adopted, because there are no clear interpretation acts. An example is the issue of secondary pledge. Such a pledge is recognized under the Civil Code. However, there is no further explanation as to how it is enforced. Therefore, the courts to date (1998) have usually refused to accept secondary pledge.

§2. Historical Background

19. Vietnam was later than Western countries in developing its Intellectual Property Law (IPL). Not earlier than 1957, the Republic of Vietnam (the Saigon Regime) adopted the Trade Mark Law, and in 1958, the Democratic Republic of Vietnam (now the Socialist Republic of Vietnam) adopted the Rules on Commercial Products and Trade Names. In 1976, Vietnam joined the World Intellectual Property Organization (WIPO). On 14 December 1982, the Ministers' Council issued Decree No. 197/ HĐBT on Trademark Regulations. Having said this, the Vietnamese government has paid close attention to intellectual property from the early days of its establishment. Vietnam established the Science State Committee in 1959, which was then reformed in 1975 to become the State Patent Agency, which later became the National Office of Industrial Property (NOIP). In 2003, the NOIP was reformed again to become the NOIP. The establishment and operation of the NOIP have had a very important role in developing IPL regulations in Vietnam.

20. Since the Doi Moi policy, the Communist party has paid closer attention to IPL. The principle of intellectual property protection was entered into the Constitution 1992 as follows: Citizens have the right to pursue scientific and technology research, create inventions, innovations, and creative works, and participate in other cultural activities. The state protects copyrights and industrial property rights. As noted, before 1992, many regulations involving intellectual property rights had been developed as the legal basis for Doi Moi policy, such as Trademark Regulations of 14 February 1982, Industrial Design of 13 May 1988, Offshore Technology Transfer Ordinance of 5 December 1988, Decree No. 49/HĐBT of 4 March 1991 implementing Offshore Technology Transfer Ordinance, Industrial Property Protection Ordinance of 11 February 1989, Decree No. 84/HĐBT of 20 March 1990 implementing Industrial Property Protection Ordinance, Technology Licensing Regulations of 28 December 1984, Decree No. 214/HĐBT on Copyright of 1988, Copyright Protection Ordinance of 10 February 1994. However, there were still inconsistencies in intellectual property rights protection between the central economy before Doi Moi and the market economy after Doi Moi.

21. As society develops, requirements for intellectual property rights evolve. On 28 October 1995, The IX National Assembly, at the 8th Plenary Session, adopted the Civil Code of Vietnam, in which Part VI regulates intellectual properties, and Part VII regulates technology transfer. Following the adoption of the Civil Code, a number of implementing regulations have been issued, including:

(1) Decree No. 63/CP of 24 October 1996 on industrial property rights (amended by Decree No. 06/2001/NĐ-CP of 1 February 2001).
(2) Decree No. 76/CP of 29 November 1996 on copyright.
(3) Decree No. 31/2001/NĐ-CP of 26 June 2001 on administrative penalization in cultural and information matters.
(4) Decree No. 45/1998/NĐ-CP of 8 July 1998 on technology transfer.
(5) Decree No. 16/2000/NĐ-CP of 10 June 2000 on administrative penalization in technology transfer.
(6) Decree No. 12/1999/NĐ-CP of 6 March 1999 on administrative penalization in industrial property rights.
(7) Decree No. 54/2000/NĐ-CP of 3 October 2000 on industrial property rights on trade secrets, geographical indication, trade names and protection against unfair competition in the field of industrial property rights.
(8) Decree No. 42/2003/NĐ-CP of 2 May 2003 on the protection of integrated circuit.
(9) Circular No. 23/TC-TCT of 9 May 1997 on industrial property rights registration fees.
(10) Circular No. 825/2000/TT-BKHCNMT of 3 May 2000 implementing Decree No. 12/1999/NĐ-CP on administrative penalization in industrial property rights (amended by Circular No. 49/2001/TT-BKHCNMT).
(11) Inter-Ministerial Circular No. 10/2000/TTLT-BTM-BTC-BCA- BKHCNMT implementing Instruction No. 31/1999/CT-TTg of 27 October 1999 of the Prime Minister on the combating against counterfeit goods.
(12) Circular No. 27/2001/TT-BVHTT implementing Decree No. 76/CP of 29 November 1996 on copyright.
(13) Inter-Ministerial Circular No. 01/2001/TTLT-TANDTC/BVHTT/ VKSNDTC on handling of copyright violation.
(14) Circular No. 3055/SHCN of 31 December 1996 implementing Decree No. 63/CP.
(15) Circular No. 1254/1999/TT-BKHCNMT of 20 July 1999 implementing Decree No. 45/1998/NĐ-CP.
(16) Circular No. 29/2003/TT-BKHCN of 5 November 2003 guiding the registration of industrial property rights.
(17) Circular No. 30/2003/TT-BKHCN of 5 November 2003 guiding the registration of patents and innovative solutions. In May 2005, the Civil Code of 1995 was materially amended (so-called Civil Code 2005). Civil Code 2005 replaced the Civil Code of 1995 as of 1 January 2006. Therefore, the above legislations provided only a temporary legal basis before they were replaced by The IPL 2005, amended and supplemented in 2009 (discussed below).

22. As in most civil law countries, intellectual property rights in Vietnam are divided into three groups: copyright, industrial property rights and plant variety rights. Copyright protects the creative expression of an idea, that is, a work. Industrial property rights give protection to an invention, industrial design, layout design, mark, trade names, geographical indication or trade secrets. Plant variety rights give protection to a new plant variety.

Intellectual property rights in Vietnam began with the Civil Code, but then a need for IPL was recognized. This is because intellectual property rights regulations consist not only of civil right protection but also of administrative regulations dealing with intellectual property right registration and the handling of violations. Moreover, regulations on intellectual property focus on intangible assets rather than tangible assets and as such do not fit in with other parts of the Civil Code. Lastly, the introduction of intellectual property regulations, which evolve quickly with the development of science and technology, into the Civil Code, which has a high standard of stability, presents potential difficulties in amending intellectual property rights after their introduction.

23. Therefore, in 2003, a bill of IPL was presented to the National Assembly. The first bill was drafted by the NOIP and the National Office of Copyright (NOC) and was widely debated and contributed to by scholars and businesses. In addition, many foreign organizations contributed to the draft of IPL due to the requirement that Vietnam adopt an intellectual property rights regime as a condition to join the World Trade Organization (WTO). At the X National Assembly, 10th Plenary Session, on 29 November 2005, IPL (Law No. 50/2005/QH10) was adopted by the National Assembly with almost unanimous approval (368/370), effective 1 July 2006. This is the first time Vietnam has had a codified law on intellectual property at the highest level. As such, this monograph only refers to IPL rather than the Civil Code 2005, although there are similarities and differences between the two regimes. Under Article 5 of the IPL, if there is a difference between IPL and other laws (including the Civil Code), the IPL controls. If, however, the IPL is different from an international treaty to which Vietnam is a member country, then the regulations of the international treaty shall control. At the XII National Assembly, 5th Plenary Session, on 19 June 2009, IPL was amended and supplemented by the National Assembly, effective from 1 January 2010. As such, the hierarchy of sources of intellectual property regulations are as follows:

- Constitution.
- International treaties to which Vietnam is a member country (such as TRIPS, Paris Convention or Berne Convention).
- IPL, the Civil Code and other relevant laws.

24. Under Article 221, IPL is effective from 1 July 2006. However, patents and trademark registration certificates, as well as other IP certificates granted before 1 July 2006, remain effective. Particularly, copyright and related rights effective prior to IPL remain protected under IPL if they were protected as of the effective date of IPL. Applications for registration of copyright, related rights, inventions, utility models, industrial designs, marks, appellations of origin of goods, layout designs or plant varieties which were filed with the competent bodies before the effective date of IPL shall continue to be processed in accordance with the provisions of the legal instruments effective at the date of filing. Trade secrets and trade names which existed and were protected pursuant to Decree No. 54-2000-ND-CP continue to be protected under IPL. However, geographical indications, including those protected under Decree No. 54, shall only be protected after registration in accordance with the provisions of IPL.

25. Up to now, the Law has undergone three amendments and supplements in 2009, 2019, and 2022 to comply with the international treaties that Vietnam has recently ratified, such as CPTPP, EVFTA, and RCEP. The amendments and supplements in 2022 officially came into effect on 1 January 2022.

The sub-law regulations, as of December 2023, include the following regulations:

(1) Decree 65/2023/ND-CP, detailing and guiding the implementation of the IPL regarding industrial property, protection of industrial property rights, rights to plant varieties, and state management of intellectual property.
(2) Decree 79/2023/ND-CP guides the IPL and its amendment on rights to plant varieties.
(3) Decree 129/2021/ND-CP amends decrees related to administrative penalties in the fields of tourism, sports, copyright, related rights, culture, and advertising.
(4) Decree 76/2018/ND-CP guides the Technology Transfer Law.
(5) Decree 22/2018/ND-CP provides guidance on the IPL of 2005 and its 2009 amendment regarding copyright and related rights.
(6) Decree 28/2017/ND-CP amends Decree 131/2013/ND-CP.
(7) Decree 43/2017/ND-CP concerns product labeling.
(8) Decree 131/2013/ND-CP stipulates administrative penalties for copyright and related rights violations.
(9) Decree 99/2013/ND-CP regulates administrative penalties in the field of industrial property.
(10) Decree 119/2010/ND-CP amends Decree 105/2006/ND-CP.
(11) Decree 105/2006/ND-CP guides the IPL on industrial property ownership.
(12) Decree 31-CP of 1981 regulates technical innovation and rationalization of production and invention, issued by the Government Council.
(13) Circular 75/2021/TT-BTC regulates financial management for implementing the Intellectual Property Asset Development Programme until 2030, issued by the Ministry of Finance.
(14) Circular 03/2021/TT-BKHCN regarding the management of the Intellectual Property Development Programme until 2030, issued by the Ministry of Science and Technology.
(15) Circular 31/2020/TT-BTC amends Circular 263/2016/TT-BTC.
(16) Circular 263/2016/TT-BTC on the rates, regimes, collection, management, and use of fees for the assessment of technology transfer contracts issued by the Ministry of Finance.
(17) Circular 13/2020/TT-BTC amends Circular 13/2015/TT-BTC.
(18) Circular 13/2015/TT-BTC on the inspection, supervision, temporary suspension of customs procedures for exported and imported goods requiring intellectual property protection, and the control of counterfeit goods and goods infringing intellectual property rights, issued by the Minister of Finance.

(19) Circular 02/2018/TT-BKHCN provides guidance on reporting regimes for the implementation of technology transfer contracts under the list of restricted technology transfers; forms of documents in activities of granting technology transfer licences, registration of extension, amendment, supplementation of technology transfer content, issued by the Minister of Science and Technology.
(20) Circular 169/2016/TT-BTC regulates the rates, regimes, collection, management, and use of fees for the appraisal of technology transfer contracts issued by the Minister of Finance.
(21) Circular 09/2015/TT-BKHCN stipulates the management of activities to enhance national scientific and technological capabilities by the National Science and Technology Development Fund, issued by the Minister of Science and Technology.
(22) Circular 04/2012/TT-BKHCN Circulars 04/2009/TT-BKHCN and 18/2011/TT-BKHCN amend Circular 01/2008/TT-BKHCN.
(23) Circular 01/2008/TT-BKHCN guiding the issuance and withdrawal of the Industrial Property Ownership Examiner Card and the Certificate of organizations eligible to engage in industrial property ownership examination activities.

Part I. Intellectual Property Law

Chapter 1. Copyright and Related Rights

§1. Sources: Legislation

26. The first draft on copyright in the Socialist Republic of Vietnam was introduced in 1970, and the first regulation was adopted under Decree No. 84/CP in 1989. Afterwards, with assistance from WIPO experts, Vietnam introduced the Copyright Protection Ordinance of 1994, introducing protection to comply with the terms of the Berne Convention, although Vietnam did not become a Berne member until October 2004. Currently, copyright protection is provided under Chapter II of the IPL and its implementing regulations.

Authors and copyright holders who directly make creative works are protected by copyright. They can be either Vietnamese or foreigners. Copyright protects both those whose works are published for the first time in Vietnam and not yet published in any other country and those whose works are protected in Vietnam pursuant to the Berne Convention or the WTO Agreement on Trade Related Aspects of Intellectual Properties (TRIPS).

§2. Subject Matter of Protection

I. Different Categories of Protected Works

27. Under Article 14 of the IPL, copyright protects all types of works where an intangible idea can be creatively expressed in a tangible form, such as:

(a) literary works, scientific works, textbooks, teaching courses and other works expressed in written language or other characters;
(b) lectures, addresses and other speeches;
(c) press works;
(d) musical works;
(e) stage works;
(f) cinematographic works and works created by a process analogous to cinematography (hereinafter all referred to as cinematographic works);
(g) art works and applied art works;
(h) photographic works;
(i) architectural works;

(j) sketches, plans, maps and drawings related to topography or scientific works;
(k) folklore and folk art works;
(l) computer programs and data collection.

28. In addition, copyright also protects derivative works, that is, the translation, modification or transformation of original works. However, they should not be prejudicial to the copyright of the original works. For example, if the work 'How to Win Friends and Influence People' by Dale Carnegie (the original work) is translated by two translators, then each translator can have a copyright on his own translation work, provided that each (i) seeks approval from the owner of the original work, and (ii) does not copy from the other translator.

A. *Works Excluded from Protection*

29. Works outside the category of copyright protection are news stories that are mere items of information; legal instruments, administrative and other documents in the judicial domain, and official translations of such documents; and processes, systems, operational methods, concepts, principles and data.

B. *Special Categories of Works*

1. Computer Software

30. Under Article 22 of the IPL, 'computer program' is defined as a set of instructions expressed in the form of commands, codes, diagrams and other forms which, when it is attached to a device operated by a computer programming language, has the ability to make the computer or device perform a task or achieve specific results. In compliance with TRIPS requirements, computer programs shall be protected the same as literary works, irrespective of whether the computer programs are expressed in the form of source codes or machine codes. All computer software protected by other TRIPS countries is also protected by the IPL. The IPL does not develop doctrines such as *look and feel*, *scene a faire*, or *essential facility* to exclude any part of the works from copyright protection.

2. Databases

31. Data collection means a set of data selected or arranged in a creative way and expressed in electronic or other forms. Copyright protection of data collections shall not extend to the protection of the data itself and must not be prejudicial to the copyrights of the data itself. It could be said that this principle is similar to the doctrine of essential facility developed in the US or Europe.

3. Others

32. The IPL also provides a special protection regime for the copyright of folklore and folk artworks. These are defined as collective creations based on the traditions of a community or individuals which reflect the ambitions of such community and are expressed in a form appropriate to the values of such community. They could be folk tales, lyrics and riddles, folk songs and melodies, folk dances, plays, rites and games, folk art products including graphics, paintings, sculptures, musical instruments, architectural models, or other artistic expressions in any material form. As Vietnam has fifty-four nations and tribes, the sources for folklore and folk artworks are quite numerous. Two of them, *Tru* Music of Hue and *Quan ho* Music of Bac Ninh, have been protected by the United Nations Educational, Social and Cultural Organization (UNESCO) as intangible World Heritage. When using folklore to make another creative work, the author of such work must cite the origins of the folklore and folk artworks and must ensure that the authentic value of such folklore and folk artworks is preserved.

§3. Conditions of Protection

I. Formal Requirements

33. Under Article 16 of the IPL, copyright arises at the moment a work is created and fixed in a material form, irrespective of its content, quality, form, mode, or language and irrespective of whether or not such work has been published or registered. Thus, a work is protected by copyright when it is created. However, Article 49 of the IPL also provides for a mechanism of voluntary registration of copyright and related rights for evidentiary purposes. Accordingly, registration of copyright and related rights entails the filing of an application by an author, copyright holder or related rights holder with the NOC in order to record information on the author, the work, the copyright holder and the related rights holder. The filing of an application for grant of a certificate of registered copyright is not a compulsory prerequisite for entitlement to copyright in accordance with the provisions of IPL. So far, most certificates of copyright registration are issued for Vietnamese enterprises and are for types of works such as labels and art works. Although a copyright registration certificate is not a prerequisite for copyright protection, the rightholders who are granted certificates of copyright have an evidentiary advantage. They are exempted from the burden of proving such copyright in a dispute unless contrary proof is tendered.

34. An application for registration of copyright starts with a declaration for registration of copyright. The declaration must be made in Vietnamese and must include complete information on the applicant, author, and copyright holder; the summarized content of the work, performance, audio and visual fixation or broadcast; the name of the author, and the title of the work used to make the derivative work if the work to be registered is a derivative work; the date, place and form of publication; and a provision accepting liability for the information set out in the application. In addition to the declaration, the declarant must attach two copies of the work he wishes to copyright, the written consent of co-authors in the case of work under joint authorship, or the written consent of co-owners if the copyright is jointly owned (Article 50 IPL).

35. The process of registration is straight forward. After the application dossier is filed with the NOC, it will grant a registered copyright certificate to the applicant or shall notify the applicant in writing in a case where it refuses to grant a certificate within a time limit of fifteen working days from the date of receipt of a valid application. Registered copyright certificates shall be officially recorded in the National Register of Copyright and Related Rights. Decisions on the grant, re-grant, renewal and cancellation of the effectiveness of registered copyright certificates and registered related rights certificates shall be published in the Official Gazette on copyright and related rights. Where the grantee of a registered copyright certificate is not the author, copyright holder or related rights holder or where the registered work, audio or visual fixation or broadcast is ineligible for protection, the NOC shall cancel the effectiveness of such certificate. Any person who discovers that the grant of a registered copyright certificate or registered related rights certificate was contrary to law shall be entitled to request the NOC to cancel the effectiveness of such a certificate.

II. Substantive Requirements

36. A work is copyrightable if it is creative; that is, it must be created personally by authors through their intellectual labour and without copying the works of others. The IPL and its implementing regulations do not specify what can become a 'creative' work and what is a 'copy' work, or indeed, what is a 'work'. Generally speaking, a work is a complete expression of idea. For example, the movie 'X-MEN' by Warner Bros is a work, but the name 'X-MEN' is not a work. When a shampoo was named 'X-MEN' by ICP, a Vietnamese consumer products company, Warner Bros took action against ICP. However, this claim was found baseless, as ICP did not violate any work from Warner Bros. Warner Bros later launched another action for trademark violation of ICP, but it too failed because ICP registered trademark X-MEN before Warner Bros did.

§4. Ownership

I. The Author (Initial Authorship) and the Copyright Holders

37. Authors who use their own time, finances and material or technical facilities to create works are vested with full copyright. If an author created works from instructions or while under contract for hire of others, the author shall have only moral rights with regard to the works (i.e., the right to be named as author, the right to name the work and the right to protect the integrity of the works) and the right to receive reward from the work. A copyright holder means a person who holds one, several or all of the economic rights stipulated in IPL. Copyright holders can be authors (if they use their own time, finance and material or technical facilities to create works), or their heirs, or their assignees of rights. In addition, the State shall be the holder of the copyright in the following works: (a) anonymous works; (b) works for which the term of protection has not expired but the copyright holder died without leaving an heir or the heir renounced the inheritance or was deprived of the right to inherit; or (c) works for which the ownership right was assigned to the State by the copyright holder.

II. Joint Works/Works Created by Several Persons

38. Under Article 38 IPL, co-authors who use their time, finance and material or technical facilities to jointly create works shall share the rights to such works. A co-author who has jointly created a work, a separate part of which is detachable for independent use without prejudice to the parts of the work of the other co-authors, has the right to such a separate part. An example of such co-authors is the poet, who is the author of a song's lyrics, and the composer, who is the author of the song's music. When it is impossible to detach the creative part of each co-author, the use of their works must be subject to their common consent.

III. Works Made for Hire

39. Vietnamese law focuses on protecting those who spend economic resources to create works rather than the authors of such works. Article 39 IPL provides that those who assign tasks to authors or who enter into contracts with authors will become the rightholders of such works (without prejudice to the moral right of the authors). Particularly, any organization which assigns the task of creating a work to an author who belongs to such organization shall be the copyright holder unless otherwise agreed. Any person who enters into a contract with an author for the creation of a work shall be the copyright holder unless otherwise agreed.

§5. Transfer

I. Assignment of Copyright

40. Assignment of copyright means the transfer by copyright holders of the ownership of the copyright to other rightholders pursuant to a contract or in accordance with a relevant provision of law. Having said this, authors shall not be permitted to assign the moral rights (except for the right of publication). Where a work is under joint ownership, its assignment must be agreed upon by all co-owners. In a case of joint ownership of a work composed of separate parts detachable for independent use, copyright holders may assign their copyright in their separate parts to other persons without prejudice to the rights of the co-owners of other parts. Under

Article 46 IPL, a contract for the assignment of copyright must be made in writing and include the following principal contents:

(a) Names and addresses of the assignor and the assignee.
(b) Grounds for the assignment.
(c) Price and method of payment.
(d) Rights and obligations of the parties.
(e) Liability for contractual breach.

The performance, amendment, termination or cancellation of a contract for the assignment of copyright must comply with the provisions of the Civil Code.

II. Licences

41. Licensing of copyright means the grant of permission by the copyright holder for another person to use for a definite term one, several or all of his or her rights stipulated in IPL. As with assignment, authors shall not be permitted to license their moral rights (except for the right of publication). Likewise, in the case of neighbouring rights, performers shall not be permitted to license their moral rights. Where a work is under joint ownership, the licensing of copyright must be agreed upon by all co-owners. In a case of joint ownership of a work composed of separate parts detachable for independent use, copyright holders may license their copyright in their separate parts to other persons; that is, the licensees. The licensee may also sub-license their rights to other rightholders after obtaining permission from the copyright holder.

42. The performance, amendment, termination or cancellation of a contract for the licensing of copyright must comply with the provisions of the Civil Code. A contract for the licensing of copyright must be made in writing and include the following principal contents:

(a) Full names and addresses of the licensor and the licensee.
(b) Grounds for the licence.
(c) Scope of the licence.
(d) Price and method of payment.
(e) Rights and obligations of the parties.
(f) Liability for contractual breach.

§6. Scope of Exclusive Rights

43. Under Article 18, copyright in works regulated in IPL shall comprise moral rights and economic rights. These rights are elaborated in detail as follows.

I. Moral Rights

44. Moral rights of authors shall comprise the rights to protect the integrity of the work. Such integrity is attached to the author and in principle is not transferable except when it is related to an economic right (i.e., the right to publish the work and the right to give titles to the work). These comprise the following rights:

(1) to give titles to their works;
(2) to attach their real names or pseudonyms to their works; to have their real names or pseudonyms acknowledged when their works are published or used;
(3) to protect the integrity of their works; and to forbid other persons to modify, edit or distort their works in whatever form, causing harm to the honour and reputation of the author; and
(4) to publish their works or to authorize other persons to publish their works. While the first three moral rights are understandable, the fourth right is related to economic rights rather than the integrity of the author. Therefore, unlike other moral rights, the publication right is transferable and can also be subject to license.

II. Exploitation Rights

45. Exploitation rights are so-called exclusive economic rights of the copyright holder with regard to his or her work. Authors or copyright holders shall exclusively exercise these rights or may grant other persons the right to exercise such rights pursuant to the provisions of IPL. When any person exercises one, several or all of these exclusive rights, such person must ask for permission from the copyright holder and must pay royalties, remuneration or other material benefits to the copyright holder. The exploitation rights are as follows.

A. Reproduction Right

46. The copyright holder has an exclusive right to reproduce the work. Reproduction also means the right to publish, copy, distribute the work, display the work to the public, distribute or import the original or copies of the work, or communicate the work to the public by wireless or landline means, electronic information networks or other technical means. This right is related to the publication right (protected under the moral right). The reproduction right also includes the right to collect royalty or other income on such reproduction right. Except for fair use (which shall be explained below), any reproduction without the consent of the copyright holder shall be deemed to be a violation of copyright.

B. Performing Right

47. The performing right is an exclusive right of the copyright holder to perform the work by any means, such as singing a song or acting at a theatre. Performing a work does not in itself amount to a copyright violation, except when such performance is for a commercial purpose. For example, reading a cookbook to make a meal is not a copyright violation. Likewise, singing a song is not a copyright violation unless such performance is for a commercial purpose. The term 'commercial purpose' should be broadly interpreted to include any form of collecting remuneration, even if such remuneration is later used for charitable purposes.

C. Adaptation Right (Including Translation Right)

48. Adaptation right is the exclusive right of the copyright holder to adapt a work in a different form (i.e., to make a derivative work), such as translate a work into a different language, adapt a literary work into a movie or theatrical work, or adapt a poem into a lyric of a song. Any person who adapts the work of a copyright holder must seek the consent of that copyright holder for the adaptation work to be protected.

D. Other Rights

1. Droit De Suite

49. Droit de suite did not exist in Vietnam until recently. Accordingly, owners of restaurants or public areas where music is played have to pay remuneration to the owners of such music works. It remains to be seen how this regulation shall be implemented in reality.

2. Public Lending Right

50. The public lending right is the right to lease original or copies of cinematographic works and computer programs. This right is effective mostly for cinematographic work. The copyright holder has the right to lease a video or a film to a theatre for a certain period. The difficulty presented by cinematographic works and dramatic works is the numerous authors and copyright holders in such works. Under Article 21 IPL, authors of these works include directors; screenwriters; cameramen; montage makers; music composers; art designers; studio sound, lighting and art designers; studio props and technical effects designers; and persons engaged in other creative jobs in the making of cinematographic works. Each of them has rights with respect to their creative part of the work. Particularly, persons who act as directors, playwrights, choreographers, music composers, art designers, stage sound designers, lighting and art stage designers, stage props and technical effects designers, and persons engaged in other creative jobs in making stage works have the moral rights for their creative parts. On the contrary, rightholders who invest finance or material and technical facilities in the production of cinematographic works and stage works shall be holders of the economic rights. These rightholders must pay royalties, remuneration or other material benefits as agreed with the authors.

§7. Limitations or Exemptions to the Scope of Copyright Protection

51. Article 25 IPL provides for fair use; that is, cases when published works may be used without having to seek permission or pay royalties or remuneration. Accordingly, published works may be used without having to seek permission or pay royalties or remuneration in the following cases (so-called fair use):

(a) Copying a work for personal research or educational purposes and not for commercial use. This does not apply in the case of copying using copying equipment.
(b) Reasonably copying a part of a work using copying equipment for individual research or educational purposes and not for commercial use.
(c) Reasonably using a work to illustrate in lectures, publications, performances, audio recordings, video recordings, or broadcasts for teaching purposes. This use may include providing it on an internal computer network with technical measures to ensure that only students and teachers in that class can access the work.
(d) Using the work in the official activities of state agencies.
(e) Properly citing a work without distorting the author's intent for commentary, introduction, or illustration in one's work; for writing articles, using in periodicals, broadcasting programmes, or documentary films.
(f) Using the work in library activities not for commercial purposes, including copying works stored in the library for preservation, provided that the copy is marked as an archival copy and access is limited according to library regulations. Copying a reasonable part of a work using copying equipment for others for research and educational purposes; copying or transmitting a preserved work for interlibrary use via a computer network, provided that the number of readers at the same time does not exceed the number of copies of the work held by the libraries mentioned above, except when the copyright owner allows it, and not applicable in cases where the work has been provided on the market in digital form.
(g) Performing works of theatre, music, dance, and other forms of artistic expression in cultural activities and non-commercial propaganda activities.
(h) Taking photographs, filming artistic works, architecture, photography, and applied art exhibited in public places to introduce the image of those works, not for commercial purposes.
(i) Importing a copy of someone else's work for personal use, not for commercial purposes.
(k) Copying by reposting in newspapers, periodicals, broadcasts, or other forms of public communication lectures, speeches, or other spoken presentations

made to the public within the appropriate scope for news and information purposes, except when the author declares copyright.

(l) Taking photos, recording, filming, and broadcasting events for the purpose of reporting news, including using audible and visible works in those events.

(m) People with disabilities who are visually impaired, people with disabilities who cannot read printed text, and other people with disabilities who cannot access the work in the usual way, caregivers and organizations may use the work according to the provisions of Article 25a of the IPL. Please note that the fair user must neither affect the normal use of such works nor cause prejudice to the rights of the author or copyright holder and must cite the author's name and the source and origin of the work. Fair use for copying mentioned above does not apply to architectural works, works of fine art, and computer programs; the compilation and selection of works.

52. In addition, Article 26 IPL also lists when published works may be used without having to seek permission, but royalties or remuneration must be paid, namely the use of a published work to make a broadcast. The royalties or remuneration to the copyright holder shall be made in accordance with Government regulations. Like other fair uses, this use must neither affect the normal use of such works nor cause prejudice to the rights of the author or copyright holder and must cite the author's name, the source and origin of the work. Note, however, that this use does not apply to cinematographic works.

§8. Duration of Protection

53. Under Article 27 IPL, moral rights under copyright (except the publication right) are protected for an indefinite term. The publication right and other economic rights vested in a work shall be protected for the whole life of the author plus fifty years after the death of the last (co)author of the work. Cinematographic works, photographic works, stage works, applied artworks, and anonymous works have a term of protection of seventy-five years from the date of first publication (or formation, if such work is not published within fifty years from the formation). Any work whose term of protection has expired pursuant to Article 27 of IPL shall belong to the public.[2] The use of public work is free, except that the integral moral rights of authors must be respected.

§9. Neighbouring Rights (Related Rights)

I. Eligible Subject Matters, Rightholders, Term of Protection

54. Neighbouring rights, or related rights, are rights attached to creative labour in relation to a work, namely the performances, the audiovisual programme or the

2. Article 43 IPL.

broadcasting programmes. Performances, audio and visual fixations, broadcasts and satellite signals carrying coded programmes shall only be protected as related rights if they are not prejudicial to copyright.

55. The rightholders eligible for protection of related rights are performers, producers of audiovisual fixations, broadcasters or investors. The performers are the actors and actresses, singers, instrumentalists, dancers and other persons who perform literary and artistic works. Producers of audio and visual fixations are those who fix for the first time the sounds and images of performances or other sounds and images. Broadcasters are those who initiate and carry out broadcasting. The investors are those who make a financial investment in or use their material and technical facilities to produce the performances, the audiovisual fixations or the broadcasting.[3]

56. Performances are protected if they are made by Vietnamese citizens, or made by foreigners in Vietnam, or are protected pursuant to an international treaty of which the Socialist Republic of Vietnam is a member. An audio and visual fixation is protected if it was made by a Vietnamese citizen or protected pursuant to an international treaty of which the Socialist Republic of Vietnam is a member. Please note that Vietnam has been a member of the Rome Convention for the protection of audiovisual works since 1997. Broadcasts and satellite signals carrying coded programmes are protected if they are made by Vietnamese citizens or protected pursuant to an international treaty of which the Socialist Republic of Vietnam is a member. As for the timing, related rights shall arise at the moment a performance, audio and visual fixation, broadcast or satellite signal carrying coded programmes is fixed or displayed without causing loss or damage to copyright until fifty years afterwards.

II. Scope of Rights

A. Rights of Performers and Investors

57. Performers who are also the investors have the moral rights and economic rights to their performances. Where performers are not also the investors, the performers have the moral rights, and the investors have the economic rights to performances. Moral rights are the rights to have the performer's name acknowledged, to protect the integrity of the imagery of the performance, and to prevent others from modifying, editing or distorting the work in any way prejudicial to the honour and reputation of the performer. Economic rights are the exclusive right to exercise or to authorize others to:

3. Article 44 IPL.

(a) formulate a live performance on audio and visual fixation;
(b) copy directly or indirectly the entirety or a part of their performance that has been shaped in a sound or visual recording by any means or form; however, there is no right to prohibit other organizations or individuals from copying the performance only to exercise other rights as prescribed by this Law; temporarily copying through a technological process during the operation of devices for transmission within a network between third parties through intermediaries or using lawful means to temporarily reproduce their performance shaped in a sound or visual recording, without independent economic purposes, and the copy is automatically erased with no possibility of recovery;
(c) broadcast, transmit to the public their performance that has not been shaped in a way accessible to the public, except when the performance is intended for broadcasting purposes;
(d) distribute, import for distribution to the public through sale or other forms of transfer of ownership other than the original, a shaped copy of their performance in a tangible form; however, there is no right to prohibit other organizations or individuals from distributing the next time, importing for distribution copies of the original, shaped copy of the performance that has been exercised or permitted to be distributed by the rights holder;
(e) commercially lease to the public the original or a copy of their shaped performance in a sound or visual recording, even after being distributed by the performer or with the performer's permission;
(f) broadcast, and transmit to the public a shaped copy of their performance, including providing the public with a shaped copy of the performance in a way that the public can access at a location and time of their choosing. Once a right is exclusive, any person who exploits or uses such right must pay remuneration to the performer or must follow the terms of any agreement where there is no relevant provision of law. Remuneration is usually made by an agreement reached with the performer or the association of performers.

B. *Rights of Producers of Audio and Visual Fixation*

58. Producers of audio and visual fixation have the exclusive right to exercise, or to authorize others to exercise, to:

(a) copy the entirety or a part of the sound or visual recording by any means or form; however, there is no right to prohibit other organizations or individuals from copying the sound or visual recording only to exercise other rights as prescribed by this Law; temporarily copy through a technological process during the operation of devices for transmission within a network between third parties through intermediaries or use lawful sound or visual recording, without independent economic purposes, and the copy is automatically erased, with no possibility of recovery;
(b) distribute, import for distribution to the public through sale or other forms of transfer of ownership other than the original, a shaped copy of their sound or visual recording in a tangible form; however, there is no right to prohibit other

organizations or individuals from distributing the next time, importing for distribution copies of the original, shaped copy of the sound or visual recording that has been exercised or permitted to be distributed by the rights holder;
(c) commercially lease to the public the original or a copy of their sound or visual recording, even after being distributed by the producer or with the producer's permission;
(d) broadcast, transmit to the public their sound or visual recording, including providing the public with a sound or visual recording in a way that the public can access at a location and time of their choosing.

Producers of an audio and visual fixation are entitled to material benefits when such recording is distributed to the public.[4]

C. Rights of Broadcasters

59. Broadcasters have the exclusive right to exercise, or to authorize others to exercise, to:

(a) broadcast, re-broadcast their broadcasting programme;
(b) directly or indirectly copy the entirety or a part of the shaped version of the broadcasting programme by any means or form; however, there is no right to prohibit other organizations or individuals from copying the broadcasting programme only to exercise other rights as prescribed by this Law; temporarily copy through a technological process during the operation of devices for transmission within a network between third parties through intermediaries or use the lawful broadcasting programme, without independent economic purposes, and the copy is automatically erased, with no possibility of recovery;
(c) formulate their broadcasting programme fixation;
(d) distribute, import for distribution to the public through sale or other forms of transfer of ownership other than the shaped version of their broadcasting programme in a tangible form; however, there is no right to prohibit other organizations or individuals from distributing the next time, importing for distribution copies of the shaped version of the broadcasting programme that has been exercised or permitted to be distributed by the rights holder.

Broadcasters are also entitled to collect fees when their broadcasts are recorded and distributed to the public.[5]

4. Article 30 IPL.
5. Article 31 IPL.

III. Fair Use

60. Related rights may be exercised without having to seek permission or pay royalties or remuneration in the following cases:[6]

(a) recording or filming a portion of a performance for educational purposes, not for commercial use or news reporting;
(b) self-copying or assisting individuals with disabilities in copying a portion of a performance, audio recording, video recording, or broadcast programme for scientific research and personal learning purposes, not for commercial use;
(c) reasonably copying a portion of a performance, audio recording, video recording, or broadcast programme for direct teaching purposes by an individual, not for commercial use, except in cases where this performance, audio recording, video recording, or broadcast programme has been publicly released for teaching purposes;
(d) properly quoting for news reporting purposes;
(e) broadcasting organizations making temporary copies for broadcast while enjoying broadcasting rights. The use of a fair user must neither affect the normal use of performances, audio and visual fixations or broadcasts nor cause prejudice to the rights of performers, producers of audio and visual fixations, or broadcasters.

61. Article 33 IPL also lists cases when related rights may be exercised without having to seek permission but when royalties or remuneration must be paid. This is when the users directly or indirectly use published audio and visual fixations for commercial purposes in making broadcasts which are sponsored, contain advertisements or collect fees in any form, or when they use published audio and visual fixations in business or commercial activities. The users in these cases must neither affect the normal use of performances, audio and visual fixations or broadcasts; nor cause prejudice to the rights of performers, producers of audio and visual fixations or broadcasters.

§10. Infringement and Remedies

62. Conduct constituting infringement of copyright includes one or more of the following:[7]

(1) Violating moral rights as stipulated in Article 19 of IPL.
(2) Violating property rights as specified in Article 20 of IPL.
(3) Failing to fulfil or inadequately fulfilling the obligations when utilizing fair use.

6. Article 32 IPL.
7. Article 28 IPL.

(4) Intentionally nullifying or disabling effective technological measures implemented by the author, copyright owner to protect their copyright concerning their works to carry out acts of copyright and related rights infringement.
(5) Producing, distributing, importing, offering for sale, selling, promoting, advertising, marketing, leasing, or storing for commercial purposes devices, products, or components, introducing or providing services when knowing or having reason to know that such devices, products, components, or services are produced, used to circumvent effective technological measures protecting copyright.
(6) Intentionally deleting, removing, or altering management information without authorization from the author, copyright owner when knowing or having reason to know that such actions will induce, create the possibility, create favourable conditions, or conceal acts infringing copyright as regulated by law.
(7) Intentionally distributing, importing for distribution, broadcasting, transmitting, or providing to the public copies of works when knowing or having reason to know that the rights management information has been deleted, removed, or altered without permission from the copyright owner; when knowing or having reason to know that such actions will induce, create the possibility, create favourable conditions, or conceal acts infringing copyright as regulated by law.
(8) Failing to fulfil or inadequately fulfilling the regulations to be exempted from legal liability of intermediary service providers as stipulated in Clause 3 of Article 198b of IPL.

63. Conduct constituting infringement of related rights is one or more of the following:[8]

(1) Violating the rights of performers as stipulated in Article 29 of IPL.
(2) Violating the rights of producers of sound recordings and video recordings as specified in Article 30 of IPL.
(3) Violating the rights of broadcasting organizations as stipulated in Article 31 of IPL.
(4) Failing to fulfil or inadequately fulfilling the obligations specified in Articles 32 and 33 of IPL.
(5) Intentionally nullifying or disabling effective technological measures implemented by the related rights owner to protect their rights in order to carry out acts of copyright and related rights infringement.
(6) Producing, distributing, importing, offering for sale, selling, promoting, advertising, marketing, leasing, or storing for commercial purposes devices, products, or components, introducing or providing services when knowing or having reason to know that such devices, products, components, or services are produced, used to circumvent effective technological measures protecting related rights.

8. Article 35 IPL.

(7) Intentionally deleting, removing, or altering management information without authorization from the related rights owner when knowing or having reason to know that such actions will induce, create the possibility, create favourable conditions, or conceal acts infringing related rights as regulated by law.
(8) Intentionally distributing, importing for distribution, broadcasting, transmitting, or providing to the public performances, copies of performances that have been shaped or audio recordings, video recordings, broadcasting programmes when knowing or having reason to know that the rights management information has been deleted, removed, or altered without permission from the related rights owner; when knowing or having reason to know that such actions will induce, create the possibility, create favourable conditions, or conceal acts infringing related rights as regulated by law.
(9) Producing, assembling, modifying, distributing, importing, exporting, offering for sale, selling, or leasing devices, systems when knowing or having reason to know that such devices, systems decrypt unauthorized signals or are primarily designed to assist in the unauthorized decryption of encrypted satellite signals carrying programmes.
(10) Intentionally receiving or continuing to distribute decrypted satellite signals without the permission of the lawful distributor.
(11) Failing to fulfil or inadequately fulfilling the regulations to be exempted from legal liability of intermediary service providers as stipulated in Clause 3 of Article 198b of IPL.

§11. Overlapping and Relation to Other Intellectual Property Laws

64. In theory, copyright does not overlap with other intellectual property rights because it protects the expression of ideas rather than the ideas themselves (such as patents or industrial designs). However, the differences between 'expression' and 'ideas' are not great; therefore, in many instances, such protection may overlap. For example, a mark could be protected as a trademark or alternatively could be protected by copyright if it could be considered an expression of an idea. Likewise, the design of a car could be protected as an industrial design or a copyrighted work. This overlap has created disputes between products. One example is the aromatic cream 'BENGAZ', which is protected by trademark, and the same product but with the mark 'BENGAY', which is registered at NOC as a copyrighted work. The court in this case gave priority protection to the trademark holder because the copyrighted work came later than the trademark.

Chapter 2. Patents

§1. Sources: Legislation

65. Invention means a technical solution in the form of a product or process which is intended to solve a problem by application of natural laws.[9] Inventions and their form of protection – patents – are protected under Chapter 3 of IPL and implemented under Decree No. 65/2023/ND-CP of 23 August 2023, detailing and guiding the implementation of the IPL regarding industrial property, protection of industrial property rights, rights to plant varieties, and state management of intellectual property. In addition, Vietnam is also a member of the Paris Convention, the Patent Cooperation Treaty (PCT) for international registration of patents, the TRIPS Agreement and the Vietnam–US Bilateral Trade Agreement, whereby a chapter (Chapter III of the Trade Agreement) also provides protection for patents. As a low-income country, it is not surprising that the number of patents in Vietnam is much less than in other countries. The following statistic proves this assessment:

Granted Patents from 1981–20021

Year	*Patent Granted For*		
	Vietnamese	*Foreigners*	*Total*
1981–1989	74	7	81
1990	11	3	14
1991	14	13	27
1992	19	16	35
1993	3	13	16
1994	5	14	19
1995	3	53	56
1996	4	58	62
1997	0	111	111
1998	5	343	348
1999	13	322	335
2000	10	620	630
2001	7	776	783
2002	9	734	743
2003	17	757	774
2004	22	676	698
2005	27	641	668
2006	44	625	669

9. Article 4.12 IPL.

Granted Patents from 1981–20021			
Year	*Patent Granted For*		
	Vietnamese	*Foreigners*	*Total*
2007	34	691	725
2008	39	627	666
2009	29	677	706
2010	29	793	822
2011	40	945	985
2012	45	980	1025
2013	59	1203	1262
2014	36	1332	1368
2015	63	1325	1388
2016	76	1347	1423
2017	109	1636	1745
2018	205	2014	2219
2019	169	2451	2620
2020	139	4180	4319
2021	153	3538	3691
Total	1,512	2,9521	3,1033

Source: National Office of Intellectual Property.[10]

The trend shows that the grant of patents from Vietnam is still not stable and that Vietnamese, a population of approximately 100 million people, have not paid close attention to patent registration. Even foreigners have not seen patent infringement as a major issue in Vietnam so that they must register patents for their products. This also means that the sources of patent information available in Vietnamese are still rare, widening the gap between the Vietnamese level and the world level over time.

§2. Patentable Subject Matter

66. Under Article 58 IPL, an invention is eligible for protection in the form of the grant of an invention patent when it satisfies the following conditions: novelty, inventive steps, and eligibility for industrial application. These definitions are in line with the minimum requirements for protection under the Paris Convention and the TRIPS Convention. Please note that there are certain subject matters that are ineligible for patent protection. These are:

10. Ipvietnam.gov.vn.

(1) scientific discoveries or theories, mathematical methods (including software programs per se, unless such software is protected under business method);
(2) schemes, plans, rules and methods for performing mental acts, training domestic animals, playing games and doing business; computer programs;
(3) presentations of information;
(4) solutions of aesthetic characteristics only;
(5) plant varieties, animal breeds;
(6) processes of plant or animal production which are principally of a biological nature, other than microbiological processes;
(7) human and animal disease prevention methods, diagnostic and treatment methods. In other words, anything new and inventive made under the sun, except for the above subject matters, using natural resources, could be protected by patent.

§3. Conditions of Patentability

I. Novelty of Inventions

67. An invention is deemed novel if it has not yet been (i) publicly disclosed by use, by means of a written description or any other form either inside or outside Vietnam before the filing date or the priority date, as applicable, of the invention registration application, and (ii) publicly disclosed in another patent application that has an earlier filing or priority date but is published on or after the filing or priority date of that patent application. Having said this, an invention is deemed not yet publicly disclosed if it is known to only a limited number of persons who must keep it secret.

68. Moreover, an invention shall not be deemed to have lost its novelty if it is it is publicly disclosed by the person who has the right to register or the person who has obtained information about the invention directly or indirectly from that person, provided that the patent application is filed at Vietnam within twelve months from the date of disclosure.

II. Inventive Nature of Inventions

69. An invention is deemed to be of an inventive nature if, based on technical solutions already publicly disclosed by use or by means of a written description or any other form either inside or outside Vietnam prior to the filing date or the priority date as applicable of the application for registration of the invention, the invention constitutes inventive progress and cannot be easily created by a person with average knowledge in the art.

III. Inventions Which Are Susceptible to Industrial Application

70. An invention is deemed to be susceptible to industrial application if it is possible to both realize mass manufacturing or production of products or repeated application of the process which is the subject matter of the invention, and to achieve stable results.

§4. Formalities (Procedure for Grant and Obtaining Patent Protection)

I. First to File Principle and Priority Date

71. Vietnamese or foreigners residing in Vietnam or having subsidiaries/permanent establishment in Vietnam can file patent applications either directly or through patent agents in Vietnam. Other foreigners must file patent applications through patent agents in Vietnam.

Vietnam follows the 'First to file' principle, which means, where two or more applications are filed which are identical or insignificantly different from each other, a protection title may only be granted to the earliest valid application. The date of application is called the 'priority date' (unless another priority date under the Paris Convention is claimed, as discussed in the paragraph below). Where there are two or more applications satisfying all the conditions for the grant of a protection title and having the same priority or filing date, a protection title may only be granted to one of the applications and with agreement from all applicants in question. Without such an agreement, all such applications are refused the grant of a protection title.

72. The first to file principle applies not only to patent application but also to industrial design and mark. For this principle to apply, the first application must be filed in Vietnam or in a Paris Convention country containing provisions on first to file priority principle. Moreover, the applicant must be a citizen of a Paris Convention country. The applicant must state a claim of priority right in the application, to be attached with a copy of the first application certified by the receiving patent office. Moreover, the application must be filed within the time limit provided by a treaty of which Vietnam is a member, namely twelve months from the first application if the priority is sought under the Paris Convention. The similarity between the contents of such earlier applications and the present application must also be indicated in the application. Once the priority date under the Paris Convention is recognized, the application shall deem such a priority date to be the filing date of the first application.

II. General Requirements for Application

73. A patent registration application shall contain a declaration for registration, samples and information identifying the invention to be registered for protection, documents evidencing the application right (if such right is acquired by the applicant from another eligible person), documents evidencing the priority right (if applicable), a power of attorney (if applicable), and receipt for payment of fees and charges. All application documents must be made in Vietnamese or translated into Vietnamese.

74. Authorization for carrying out procedures related to the establishment, maintenance, extension, amendment, termination and invalidation of protection titles must be made in writing in the form of a power of attorney. The power of attorney should contain the full name and address of the principal and of the attorney, the scope of authorization, the validity of authorization, the date the power of attorney was made and the signature and seal (if any) of the principal. A power of attorney without any limiting terms is considered valid indefinitely and is terminable by the principal at will.

75. Under Article 108 IPL, an application for registration of industrial property (including patents) shall only be received by NOIP for industrial property rights if the application consists of at least the following documents and information:

(a) A declaration for registration of a patent, industrial design, layout design, mark or geographical indication, which includes sufficient information to identify the applicant and, in the case of a mark, a sample of the mark and a list of goods or services bearing the mark.
(b) A description, including the scope of protection, in the case of an application for registration of a patent; a set of photos and drawings and a description in the case of an application for registration of an industrial design; and a description of the peculiar characteristics of a product bearing a geographical indication, in the case of an application for registration of a geographical indication.
(c) A receipt for payment of the filing fee.

76. The filing date is the date on which the application is received by NOIP for industrial property rights or the international filing date in the case of an application filed pursuant to an international treaty, such as the Paris Convention or the PCT.

Before NOIP grants or refuses to grant a protection title, the applicant has the right to make a written declaration withdrawing the application. Once an applicant declares withdrawal of the application, all further procedures related to such application shall cease and fees and charges already paid in relation to procedures which have not yet commenced are refunded to the applicant at his or her request. Withdrawn applications are deemed not to have been filed, except where they serve as grounds for claims for priority right.

III. Patent Description, Abstract and Claims

77. Each patent registration application should be limited to a single patent or one utility model patent (a kind of simple patent) for a group of inventions that are technically linked to form a single common inventive idea. Documents identifying an invention registered for a patent must include a description of the invention and an abstract of the invention. The invention description shall contain a descriptive section and the scope of protection of the invention. The description of an invention must satisfy the following conditions:

(a) Fully and clearly disclose the nature of the invention so that it is recognizable by a person with average knowledge in the field.
(b) Briefly explain accompanying drawings if such an explanation is required to clarify the nature of the invention.
(c) Clarify the novelty, inventive steps and susceptibility of industrial application of the invention.

78. The scope of protection of an invention (the patent claim) must be expressed in the form of a combination of technical specifications which are necessary and sufficient to identify the scope of the rights to such invention, compatible with the description of the invention and the drawings. An abstract of an invention must disclose the principal features of the invention. Normally, the abstract shall not be longer than three hundred words, which shall later be published in the IP Official Gazette.

IV. Formal Examination

79. Applications for registration of industrial property (including patents) are subject to formal examination for evaluation of their validity within one month from the filing date. For this purpose, an application for registration of industrial property is considered invalid in the following cases:

(a) It does not fulfil the formal requirements.
(b) The subject matter stated in the application is ineligible for protection.
(c) The applicant does not have the registration right, including where the registration right belongs to more than one person, but one or more of them does not agree to the filing.
(d) The application is filed in contravention of filing method regulations stipulated in section A above.
(e) The applicant fails to pay fees and charges.

80. For invalid applications, NOIP shall:

(a) issue a notice of intended refusal to accept the invalid application, clearly stating the reasons and setting a time limit (normally sixty days) for the applicant to correct errors or to object to such intended refusal;
(b) issue a notice of refusal to accept the invalid application if the applicant fails to correct errors, improperly corrects errors or fails to make a justifiable objection to such intended refusal;

(c) issue a notice of refusal to grant a certificate of registered design of semi- conducting closed circuits in case of a closed circuit registration application;
(d) accept the application if the applicant properly corrects errors or makes a justifiable objection to the intended refusal to accept the invalid application.

For valid applications, NOIP shall issue a notice of acceptance of the valid application or carry out procedures for granting a protection title and recording it in the National Register of Industrial Property.

V. Publication and Opposition Period

81. Under Article 110 IPL, applications accepted as being valid by NOIP are published in the Official Gazette of Industrial Property. Particularly, applications for patent registration are published during the nineteenth month after the filing date or the priority date, as applicable, or at an earlier time at the request of the applicant. Before applications for patent registration and industrial designs are published in the Official Gazette of Industrial Property, NOIP must keep the information therein confidential. State employees of NOIP who disclose information in applications for patent registration and industrial designs are disciplined and may also be responsible for damages. An opposition period is provided under Article 112 IPL. From the date an application for registration of industrial property is published in the Official Gazette of Industrial Property until the date a decision on the grant of a protection title is issued, any third party has the right to express an opinion to NOIP on the grant or refusal to grant a protection title for such application. Such opinions must be made in writing and must either quote the source of the information or be accompanied by documentation.

VI. Substantive Examination

82. Within forty-two months after the filing date or the priority date, as applicable, an applicant or any third party may request that NOIP substantively examine an application for registration of a patent. The requesting party must pay a substantive examination fee. Please note that where no request for substantive examination is filed within this time limit, the patent application will be deemed withdrawn. The time limit for making a request for substantive examination of an application for registration of a patent involving a request for a utility model patent is thirty-six months from the filing date or the priority date, as applicable.

83. Substantive examination is an evaluation of the eligibility of a particular application for a grant of protection title under protection conditions and for determination of the respective scope of protection. For substantive examination to be performed, an application for patent registration must already have been accepted as valid, and the request for substantive examination must be filed in accordance with regulations. The time limit for substantive examination of a patent application is eighteen months from the date of its publication (if a request for substantive examination is filed before the date of publication of the application) or from the date of receipt of a request for substantive examination (if such request is filed after the date of publication of the application).

84. During the substantive examination period, an applicant may send a request to NOIP, with additional fees and charges, to amend or supplement the application; to divide the application; to request the recording of changes in the name or address of the applicant; to request the recording of change of applicant as a result of application transfer under a contract, bequest or inheritance, or under a decision of a competent agency; or to convert an application for registration of a patent involving a request for a patent into an application for registration of a patent involving a request for a utility model patent, and vice versa. The filing date of a divided application is deemed to be the filing date of the original application.

In accordance with the uniformity principle of application, any amendment or supplementation of an application for registration of industrial property must neither change the nature of nor expand the scope of the subject matter already disclosed or stated in the application.

VII. International Application

85. Applications for registration of industrial property filed pursuant to a treaty to which the Socialist Republic of Vietnam is a member, such as the PCT, are international applications. International applications and the processing thereof must comply with these relevant treaties. In Vietnam, the application shall be made at the NOIP in the form provided by the WIPO and shall include the national and international fees. When international applications appoint Vietnam as a country of substantive examination, the order and procedure for processing follow the principles stipulated in Chapter III (patents) of the IPL.

VIII. Refusal to Grant a Patent

86. NOIP may refuse to grant a patent, or any industrial property, in the following cases:

(a) There are grounds to affirm that the subject matter stated in the application does not fully satisfy the conditions for protection.
(b) The application satisfies the conditions for the grant of a protection title but does not have the earliest filing date or priority date.
(c) The application involves a patent invented by many inventors/investors who are eligible to be patent applicants but lack the consensus of all eligible applicants.

87. When an application is refused, NOIP shall notify the applicant(s) of its intended refusal to grant a protection title, clearly stating the reasons and setting a time limit for the applicant to make an objection to such intended refusal. If the applicant makes no objection or makes unjustifiable objections to such intended refusal, the NOIP shall send another notice that makes the refusal effective. Otherwise, if the applicant has made a justifiable objection to the intended refusal, the NOIP will grant a protection title and record it in the National Register of Industrial Property. Where an objection is made to the intended grant of a protection title, the relevant application for registration of industrial property is re-examined with regard to the matters about which the objection is made. The time limit for re-examination of an application for registration of the industrial property is equal to two-thirds of the time limit for the initial examination. In complicated cases, the time limit may be extended, but it must not exceed the time limit for the initial examination. The duration for amendment or supplementation of applications shall not be included in this time limit.

IX. Grant a Patent

88. Where an application for registration of industrial property does not warrant refusal to grant protection, and the applicant has paid the fee, NOIP will grant a protection title and enter it in the National Register of Industrial Property. The name of the owner is stated in the patent. In addition, the patent also states the author of the patent, the subject matter, scope and term of protection. The owner of a protection title may request that NOIP make amendments to the following information in such protection title: changes/corrections of errors to the name and address of the author or the protection title owner, amendments to the description of a particular characteristic, quality or geographical area bearing a geographical indication; amendments to the regulations on use of collective marks or the regulations on use of certification marks. In addition, at the request of the owner of a protection title, NOIP must correct errors which are its own fault in such a protection title. The owner of a protection title may also request NOIP to narrow the scope of industrial property rights. In such a case, the corresponding industrial property registration application is substantively re-examined, and the requesting party shall pay a fee for substantive examination.

89. Decisions on the grant of protection titles, the principal contents of protection titles and decisions on the amendment, termination of validity or cancellation of validity of protection titles, as well as decisions regarding registration of industrial property right transfer contracts, shall all be recorded in the National Register of Industrial Property. The National Register of Industrial Property refers to the document recording the establishment, change and transfer of industrial property rights to inventions, industrial designs, layout designs, marks and geographical indications pursuant to IPL. The National Register of Industrial Property is compiled and kept by NOIP. Likewise, decisions on the grant, termination of validity, cancellation of validity or amendment of protection titles for industrial property rights are published by NOIP in the Official Gazette of Industrial Property within sixty days from the date of issuance of such decision.

§5. OWNERSHIP AND TRANSFER (ASSIGNMENT: LICENCES)

I. Eligible Applicants and Owners

90. The right to register inventions shall belong to authors who have created inventions by their own labour and at their own expense, or people who have supplied funds and material facilities to authors in the form of job assignment or hiring, unless otherwise agreed by the parties involved. A person who has the registration right as stipulated in this article may assign such right to other persons by a written contract, bequest or inheritance, even where a registration application has already been filed.

If the inventions are created by using material and technical facilities and funds from the State Budget, then the State shall have the right to register such inventions, or become the co-owner of the patents of such inventions, if they are created partly from the State Budget. Where a number of rightholders have jointly created or invested in the creation of an invention, industrial design or layout design, such rightholders shall all have the registration right which may only be exercised with the consensus of all.

91. The eligible applicants, once granted the patents, shall become the patent owners. However, the law also provides protection to the inventors, that is, those who have personally created the patent. Where two or more persons have jointly created an industrial property object, they are co-authors of it. These authors shall enjoy moral rights, both to be named as authors in the patents or utility model patents and to be acknowledged as authors in documents in which inventions are published or introduced. Moreover, authors shall also enjoy economic rights to receive remuneration.

II. Assignment of Patents

92. Patent assignment (or patent transfer of ownership) must be established in the form of a written contract. Under the rule *nemo plus iuris plus quam ipse habeat*, the right owners may only assign their rights within the scope of protection, and the contract must contain the following principal contents:

(1) Full names and addresses of the assignor and of the assignee.
(2) Grounds for the assignment.
(3) Assignment price.
(4) Rights and obligations of the assignor and the assignee.

93. A patent assignment contract is valid upon its registration with NOIP. An application file for registration of a patent licence contract shall contain:

(1) A declaration for registration made according to the sample form.
(2) The original or a valid copy of the contract.

(3) The original protection title in the case of an industrial property right assignment.
(4) The co-owners' written consent, or a written explanation of the reason for disagreement of any co-owner with the right assignment where the industrial property right is under joint ownership.
(5) Receipt for payment of fees and charges.
(6) A power of attorney if the application is filed by a representative.

Regulations on the order and procedures for receiving and processing application files for registration of patent licence contracts and for industrial property right assignment contracts are provided in Decree No. 65/2023/ND-CP dated 23 August 2023, detailing and guiding the implementation of the IPL regarding industrial property, protection of industrial property rights, rights to plant varieties, and state management of intellectual property.

III. Licensing of Patents

94. Patent licensing is the grant of permission by the owner of such patent for another person to use the patent within the scope of the owner's right. The licence must be established in the form of a written contract. The licensee must not enter into a sub-licence contract with a third party unless permitted to by the licensor.

Patent licensees under exclusive contracts must use such patents in the same manner as the patent owners.

Patent licence contracts can be one of the following types:

(1) Exclusive contract means a contract under which, within the licensing scope and term, the licensee has the exclusive right to use the licensed patent. For the duration of an exclusive contract, the licensor may neither enter into any patent licence contract with any third party nor, without permission from the licensee, use the patent.
(2) Non-exclusive contract means a contract under which, within the licensing scope and term, the licensor retains the right to use the patent and to enter into a non-exclusive patent licence contract with others.
(3) Patent sub-licence contract means a contract under which the licensor is a licensee of the right to use such patent pursuant to another contract.

A patent licence contract must contain the following principal contents:

(a) Full names and addresses of the licensor and of the licensee.
(b) Grounds for licensing.
(c) Contract type.
(d) Licensing scope, including limitations on use rights and territorial limitations.
(e) Contract term.
(f) Licensing price.
(g) Rights and obligations of the licensor and of the licensee.

95. Unlike a patent assignment, IPL pays attention to the protection of licensees from lack of knowledge and abuse of patent owners. Accordingly, the patent licence contract must not have provisions which unreasonably restrict the rights of the licensee. In particular, IPL prohibits the following contract provisions, which do not derive from the rights of the licensor:

(a) Prohibiting the licensee from improving the industrial property object, except for marks; compelling the licensee to transfer free of charge to the licensor improvements of the industrial property object made by the licensee or the right of industrial property registration or industrial property rights to such improvements.
(b) Directly or indirectly restricting the licensee from exporting goods produced or services provided under the patent licence contract to territories where the licensor neither holds the respective industrial property right nor has the exclusive right to import such goods.
(c) Compelling the licensee to buy all or a certain percentage of raw materials, components or equipment from the licensor or a third party designated by the licensor, unless for the purpose of ensuring the quality of goods produced or services provided by the licensee.
(d) Prohibiting the licensee from complaining about or initiating lawsuits with regard to the validity of the industrial property rights or the licensor's right to license.

Any clauses in a contract falling into the above cases are automatically invalid.

A patent licence contract is valid as agreed upon by the parties involved but is legally effective against a third party only upon registration with NOIP. The validity of a patent licence contract is automatically terminated upon termination of the licensor's patent rights.

§6. Rights and Obligations of Patent Owners, the Patent, Entry into National Registry

I. Rights of the Patent Owners: Provisional Rights

96. Patent owners have the exclusive right to use or authorize others to use their patents, to prevent others from using their patents without their permission (except when provisions of limited use apply) and to dispose of their patents by way of assignment or licensing. The use of patents includes the following acts:

(a) Manufacturing the protected product.
(b) Applying the protected process.
(c) Exploiting uses of the protected product or the product manufactured under the protected process.
(d) Circulating, advertising, offering or stocking for circulation the patent products.
(e) Importing the patented products.

Patent owners have the right to prevent others from using their patents unless such use falls into the cases of limited uses, prior use, or use under compulsory licensing (*see* Chapter 2 §7 below).

II. Provisional Rights to Inventions

97. Where an applicant for registration of a patent knows that such invention is being used by another person for commercial purposes without a prior use right, the applicant may notify in writing the user of the filing of the application for registration, clearly specifying the filing date and the date of publication of the application in the Official Gazette of Industrial Property so that the user may either terminate or continue such use. If the notified person continues using such invention, then once an invention patent is granted, the patent owner has the right to request that the user pay compensation equivalent to the price of licensing the invention, industrial design or layout design within the corresponding scope and duration of use.

III. Obligations to Pay Remuneration to Inventors

98. Under Article 135 IPL, patent owners must pay remuneration to the inventors as agreed by the parties. If the parties have no agreement on remuneration, patent owners must pay to the inventors at least 10% of the before-tax profit gained by the owner from the use of the patents or 15% of the before-tax licence fee throughout the term of protection of such patent. If there is more than one inventor, this remuneration shall be shared among them. The same rule also applies to industrial designs and layout designs.

§7. Limitations and Exceptions to the Scope of Patent Protection: Compulsory Licences

99. In general, industrial property rights may be limited pursuant to IPL by the following factors:

(1) Right of prior users to inventions or industrial designs, as well as other limited uses (such as exhaustion of rights, non-commercial use, use in transit).
(2) Obligations of owners, including:
  (a) to pay remuneration to the inventors, industrial designs or layout designs;
  (b) to use inventions or marks.
(3) Licensing of inventions pursuant to decisions of competent State bodies (compulsory licensing).

As such, patent owners must manufacture protected products or apply protected processes to satisfy the requirements of national defence and security, disease prevention, and treatment and nutrition of the people or to meet other urgent social needs. When the needs stipulated in this clause arise but an invention owner fails to perform such obligations, the competent State body may license such invention to others without permission from the invention owner.[11]

I. Prior Use

100. Prior use is a situation where a person has used or prepared necessary conditions for the use of an invention identical to the protected invention stated in such application for registration but created independently before the publication date of an application for registration of a patent. In this situation, after a protection title is granted, such person is entitled to continue using such invention within the scope and volume of use or use preparations without having to obtain permission or pay compensation to the owner of the protected invention. The exercise of the right of prior use of inventions or industrial designs shall not be deemed an infringement of the right of the owner of the invention.

To enjoy this prior use right, the user must not assign such right to others, except where such right is assigned together with the transfer of a business or production establishment which has used or has prepared to use the invention. Prior use right holders must not expand the use scope and volume unless permitted to by the owner of the invention.

II. Other Limited Uses: Non-commercial Use, Exhaustion of Rights, Use in Transit

101. Apart from prior use, patent owners may not prevent others from performing the following acts:[12]

(a) Using inventions in service of their personal needs or for non-commercial purposes, for purposes of evaluation, analysis, research, teaching, testing, trial production or information collection or for carrying out procedures of application for licences for production, importation or circulation of products.
(b) Circulating, importing, and exploiting the utility of products by the owner, the person to whom the right of use is transferred, including the transfer of usage rights under mandatory decisions, and the person with prior rights to the industrial property subject according to the provisions of this Law, to bring to the market, including foreign market.
(c) Using inventions, industrial designs or layout designs only for the purpose of maintaining the operation of foreign means of transport in transit or temporarily staying in the territory of Vietnam.

11. Article 136 IPL.
12. Article 125.2 IPL.

III. Dependent Invention

102. A dependent invention means an invention created based on another invention (hereinafter referred to as the principal invention) and may only be used if the principal invention is also used. Where the owner of a dependent invention can prove that his or her invention makes an important technical advance as compared with the principal invention and has great economic significance, he or she may request the owner of the principal invention to license such principal invention at a reasonable commercial price and with reasonable conditions. Where the owner of a principal invention fails to satisfy the request of the owner of a dependent invention without a justifiable reason, the State body concerned may license such invention to the owner of the dependent invention without permission from the owner of the principal invention, in accordance with the provisions of compulsory licence (Articles 145 and 146 of IPL).

IV. Public Use

103. Ministries and ministerial equivalent bodies have the right, on behalf of the State, to use or permit other persons to use inventions in domains under their respective management for public and non-commercial purposes, national defence and security, disease prevention, treatment and nutrition of the people, and to meet other urgent social needs without having to obtain the permission of invention owners or their licensees under exclusive contracts (hereinafter referred to as 'holders of the exclusive right to use inventions') by way of compulsory licence. Please note that the use of such inventions is limited within the scope of and under the conditions for licensing provided for compulsory licence,[13] except where such inventions are created by using material and technical facilities of the State or funds from the State Budget.

V. Grounds for Compulsory Licensing of Inventions

104. In the following cases, the right to use an invention may be licensed to another person pursuant to a decision of a competent State authority without permission from the holder of the exclusive right to use such invention:

(a) where the use of such invention is for public and non-commercial purposes or in service of national defence and security, disease prevention, treatment and nutrition of people or other urgent needs of society;
(b) where the holder of the exclusive right to use such invention fails to fulfil the obligation to use such invention under the principle of public use[14] after four years from the date of filing the application for registration of the invention or the expiration of three years from the grant date of the invention patent;

13. Clause 1, Art. 146 IPL.
14. *See* para. C above, Clause 1 of Art. 136 and Clause 5 of Art. 142 IPL.

(c) where a person who wishes to use the invention fails to reach an agreement with the holder of the exclusive right to use such invention or to enter into an invention licence contract, in spite of efforts made within a reasonable time to negotiate a satisfactory commercial price and set of conditions;
(d) where the holder of the exclusive right to use such invention is deemed to have performed anti-competitive practices prohibited by the law on competition;
(e) the use of inventions to meet the needs of pharmaceuticals for disease prevention and treatment of other countries that are eligible for import according to international treaties to which Vietnam is a member.

Please note that the holder of the exclusive right to use an invention may request termination of the use right when the grounds for licensing stipulated in clause 1 of this article no longer exist and are unlikely to recur, provided that such termination shall not be prejudicial to the licensee of the invention.

VI. Conditions to Grant a Compulsory Licence

105. The right to use an invention licensed pursuant to a State decision must comply with the following conditions:

(a) Such licensed use right is non-exclusive.
(b) Such licensed use right is limited to the scope and duration necessary to achieve the public use objectives. For an invention in semi-conducting technology, licensing is only for public and non-commercial purposes or for dealing with anti-competitive practices prohibited by the law on competition.
(c) The licensee must neither assign nor sub-license such right to others, except where the assignment is effected together with the transfer of the licensee's establishment.
(d) The licensee must pay the holder of the exclusive right to use the invention compensation according to the agreement between the parties; if the parties fail to reach an agreement on compensation, the compensation shall be determined according to the regulations stipulated by the Government except in cases where the right to use the invention is transferred according to a mandatory decision to import pharmaceuticals according to the mechanism of an international treaty to which Vietnam is a member and the compensation for the use of an invention transferred pursuant to a mandatory decision that has been paid in the exporting country.
(e) use rights are transferred mainly to provide for the domestic market, except for the cases where (i) the holder of the exclusive right to use the invention is considered to be committing an anti-competitive act that is prohibited according to the provisions of competition law, or (ii) the use of inventions to meet the demand for pharmaceuticals for disease prevention and treatment of other countries that are eligible for import according to international treaties to which Vietnam is a member.

In addition, for dependent patents, the right to use the licensed invention must also satisfy the following conditions:

(a) The holder of the exclusive right to use the principal invention shall also be licensed to use dependent inventions on reasonable terms.
(b) The licensee of the right to use the principal invention must not assign such right, except where the assignment is effected together with all rights to the dependent inventions.

106. The Ministry of Science and Technology is the primary competent authority to issue decisions on the licensing of inventions based on consideration of requests for compulsory licensing; when the use of a patent is urgent and for the purpose of national defence or protection of public health, ministries and ministerial equivalent bodies after consulting the opinion of the Ministry of Science and Technology, are permitted to issue decisions on compulsory licensing. The IPL is not clear as to whether the concept of 'inventions' also includes inventions that are not granted patents in Vietnam.

Decisions on licensing of inventions must set out appropriate use scope and conditions. The State body competent to decide on the licensing of an invention must also promptly notify the holder of the exclusive right to use such invention of its decision. This decision granting or refusing to license an invention may be subject to a complaint or lawsuit.

§8. Duration of Protection: Maintaining and Termination of Patent Protection

I. Duration and Termination

107. Protection titles under a patent follow the territorial principle. They are valid throughout the entire territory of Vietnam. An invention patent is valid from the grant date until the end of twenty years after the filing date. In order to maintain the validity of an invention patent or a utility model patent, the owner must pay a validity maintenance fee.

The validity of a protection title is terminated in the following cases:

(a) The owner fails to pay the stipulated validity maintenance or extension fee.
(b) The owner declares relinquishment of the industrial property rights.
(c) The owner dies without a lawful heir.

Where the owner of an invention protection title fails to pay the validity maintenance fee before the stipulated time limit, the validity of such protection title shall automatically terminate on the first day of the first valid year for which the validity maintenance fee has not been paid. NOIP shall record the termination in the

National Register of Industrial Property and publish it in the Official Gazette of Industrial Property.

When the owner of a protection title declares relinquishment of the industrial property right, NOIP will terminate the validity of such protection title from the date of receipt of the owner's declaration.

II. Cancellation of Effectiveness of a Patent

108. A patent can be entirely invalidated in the following cases:

(a) The invention registration application is filed contrary to the regulations on security control for inventions specified in Article 89a of the IPL.
(b) Patent registration application for an invention that is directly created based on genetic resources or traditional knowledge about genetic resources but does not disclose or incorrectly discloses the origin of genetic resources or traditional knowledge about genetic resources specified in that application.

109. A patent can be invalidated in whole or in part if all or part of that protection title does not meet the provisions of the IPL on registration rights, protection conditions, application amendments and supplements, invention disclosure, and first filing principle in the following cases:

(a) the applicant for registration does not have the right to register and has not been assigned the right to register the invention by the person with the right to register;
(b) the invention does not meet the protection conditions;
(c) amendments and supplements to the patent application expand the scope of the subject matter disclosed or stated in the application or change the nature of the subject matter requested for registration stated in the application;
(d) the invention is not fully and clearly disclosed to the extent that a person with average knowledge of the relevant technical field can implement the invention;
(e) the invention granted a protection certificate exceeds the scope disclosed in the initial description of the patent application;
(f) the invention does not meet the first to file principle.

110. Any person may request NOIP invalidate a protection title after paying fees and charges. The statute of limitations for exercising the right to request invalidation of a protection title is the whole patent term. Based on the findings of the examination of a request for invalidation of a protection title and the opinions of the parties involved, NOIP shall issue a decision entirely or partly invalidating the protection title or shall notify the parties of its refusal to invalidate. This shall also apply to the invalidation of international registrations of marks.

§9. INFRINGEMENT AND REMEDIES

I. Acts of Infringement: Rights of Protection

111. Use of the same invention or an invention insignificantly different from the protected invention, or any protected part thereof, within the valid term of a protection title and without permission from the owners is an infringement.[15] In addition, using inventions without paying compensation according to the provisions on provisional rights is also an infringement.[16]

To prevent infringement, the patent owner has the right to self-protection. The patent owner may exercise this right by:

(a) applying protective technological measures to provide rights management information or applying other technological measures to prevent acts of infringement;
(b) requesting the infringer terminate the infringement, make a public apology or rectification, and pay damage;
(c) requesting the competent State body deal with acts of infringement; or
(d) initiating a lawsuit at a court or a claim at an arbitration centre to protect the legitimate rights and interests of the holder.

112. Rightholders who suffer loss and damage caused by acts of infringement of intellectual property rights or who discover acts of infringement of intellectual property rights which cause loss and damage to consumers or society have the right to request the competent State body to deal with such acts. Moreover, rightholders who suffer loss and damage or who are likely to suffer loss and damage caused by acts of unfair competition have the right to request the competent State body apply the civil remedies (damages) and the administrative remedies stipulated in the law on competition.

113. Organizations and individuals who are defendants in intellectual property rights infringement lawsuits, if concluded by the Court that they did not commit an act of infringement, have the right to request the Court to force the plaintiff to pay them reasonable costs to hire a lawyer or for other expenses.

114. On the other hand, organizations and individuals who abuse intellectual property rights protection procedures and cause damage to other organizations and individuals must compensate for damages caused by the abuse, including reasonable costs to hire a lawyer. Abuse of intellectual property protection procedures includes acts that intentionally exceed the scope or objectives of these procedures.

15. Article 126 IPL.
16. Article 126 IPL.

II. Remedies to Infringement of Intellectual Property Rights

115. An infringer shall, depending upon the nature and seriousness of such infringement, be subject to civil, administrative or criminal remedies. In necessary cases, the competent State body may apply provisional urgent measures, measures to control intellectual property-related imports and exports, preventive measures and measures to secure enforcement of an administrative penalty in accordance with the provisions of IPL and other relevant laws.

116. There are many authorities competent to deal with acts of infringement of intellectual property rights, including the courts, inspectorates, market management offices, customs offices, police offices and people's committees at all levels. The application of civil and criminal remedies shall fall within the authority of the courts. In necessary cases, courts may apply provisional urgent measures stipulated by law. The application of administrative remedies shall fall within the authority of inspectorates, police offices, market management offices, customs offices and people's committees at all levels. In necessary cases, such bodies may apply preventive measures stipulated by law or measures to secure payment of administrative fines stipulated by law. Lastly, the application of measures to control intellectual property-related imports and exports shall fall within the authority of customs offices. However, the coordination among these authorities is not strong. Each of the authorities deals directly with the patent owner and patent infringer separately within their scope of authority. Therefore, they sometimes lack the information or power possessed by other authorities. For example, the court may grant damages, but its power to grant a search warrant is quite limited, whereas the trade inspectorate or the police may have this power. Therefore, the court may not have enough evidence to award damages to the right holder.

III. Intellectual Property Assessment

117. To assist the court or other enforcement authorities in their analysis of the subject matter of infringement or the range of damages, intellectual property rights holders often refer to intellectual property assessment. This means the use by competent persons of their professional knowledge and expertise to make an assessment of and conclusions on matters related to cases of infringement of intellectual property rights. This assessment may be arranged by a court or an enforcement officer or conducted at the request of the rightholders. The rightholders are entitled to request an intellectual property assessment in order to protect their legitimate rights and interests.

IV. Civil Action

118. Courts may apply the following civil remedies to deal with rightholders who have committed acts of infringement of intellectual property rights:

(1) Compulsory termination of the infringing acts.
(2) Compulsory public apology and rectification.
(3) Compulsory performance of civil obligations.
(4) Compulsory payment of damages for loss.
(5) Compulsory destruction, distribution or use for non-commercial purposes of goods, raw materials and materials, and facilities used principally for the production or trading of goods which infringed intellectual property rights, provided that such destruction, distribution or use will not affect the exploitation of rights by intellectual property right holders.

119. In a lawsuit regarding infringement of intellectual property rights, the plaintiff and defendant will each have the burden of proof with regard to specific elements.

First, the plaintiff must prove that he is the intellectual property right holder by presenting one of the following forms of evidence:

(a) Copies of the patent or an extract of the National Register of Industrial Property.
(b) Copy of the licence contract for an intellectual property object where the use right is licensed pursuant to a contract.

120. The plaintiff typically has the burden of proving acts of infringement of intellectual property rights or acts of unfair competition. However, in a lawsuit regarding infringement of the right to an invention which is a production process, the defendant bears the burden of proving that the product of the defendant was produced by a process other than the protected process in the following cases:

(a) The product made by the protected process is new.
(b) The product made by the protected process is not new, but the invention owner believes that the product of the defendant is made by the protected process and fails to identify the process used by the defendant in spite of having applied appropriate measures.

Following the principle set out in TRIPS, IPL also provides that where a party to a lawsuit regarding infringement of intellectual property rights can prove that appropriate evidence proving such party's claim is under the control of the other party and is therefore inaccessible, the former party has the right to request the court to compel the latter party to produce such evidence.[17]

V. Damages

121. When making a claim for compensation for damages, the plaintiff must prove the plaintiff's actual loss and damage and specify the basis for determining the amount of compensation for damages.

17. Article 203.5 IPL.

Loss and damage caused by acts of infringement of industrial property rights shall comprise:

(a) material loss and damage, including property loss, decrease in income and profit, loss of business opportunity, and reasonable expenses for mitigating and remedying the material damage;
(b) spiritual loss and damage, including damage to honour, dignity, prestige, reputation and other spiritual loss caused to the rightholders.

The extent of damages is determined on the basis of actual losses suffered by intellectual property rightholders due to acts of infringement of intellectual property rights.

122. Where the plaintiff proves that an act of infringement of intellectual property rights has caused the plaintiff material damage, the plaintiff has the right to request the court determine the amount of damages on one of the following bases:

(a) Total quantified material damages plus profit derived by the defendant as a result of the act of infringement of intellectual property rights, where the reduced profit amount of the plaintiff has not yet been included in total material damage.
(b) The price of licensing the intellectual property object on the premise that the defendant was licensed by the plaintiff to use the object under a licence contract within a scope corresponding to the act of infringement committed.
(c) Material damage according to other calculations proposed by intellectual property rights holders in accordance with the provisions of law.
(d) Where it is impossible to determine the amount of damages for material damage on the bases stipulated in sub-paragraph (a), (b) and (c) above, the amount of damages is set by the court depending on the extent of loss but must not exceed VND 500 million.

Where a plaintiff proves that the act of infringement of intellectual property rights caused the plaintiff spiritual damage, the plaintiff has the right to request the court to decide the amount of damages according to the extent of loss, to range from VND 5 million to VND 50 million.

In addition to the amount of damages above, an industrial property right holder shall also have the right to request the court to compel the person who has committed the act of infringement of industrial property rights to pay reasonable costs of engaging a lawyer.

VI. Preliminary Injunction (Provisional Urgent Measures)

123. Once a lawsuit is initiated, an intellectual property right holder has the right to request the court to apply provisional measures in the following cases:

(a) There is a danger of irreparable damage to such intellectual property right holders.
(b) Goods suspected of infringement of intellectual property rights or evidence related to the act of infringement of industrial property rights are likely to be dispersed or destroyed unless they are protected in time.

A court may make a decision applying provisional urgent measures at the request of an industrial property right holder before hearing the party subject to such measures.

124. The following provisional urgent measures may be applied to goods suspected of infringing intellectual property rights or to raw materials, materials, and facilities used for production or trading of such intellectual property counterfeit goods:

(a) Retention.
(b) Seizure.
(c) Sealing, prohibiting any alteration of the original state, prohibiting any movement.
(d) Prohibiting transfer of ownership.

125. Applicants for provisional urgent measures bear the burden of proving their right provided above by producing documentation and evidence of their right and of the act of suspected infringement. An applicant for provisional urgent measures must pay compensation for loss caused to a person subject to such measures in a case where the latter is found not to have infringed industrial property rights. To secure the performance of this obligation, an applicant for provisional urgent measures shall deposit security in one of the following forms:

(a) A sum of money equal to 20% of the value of the goods subject to the application of provisional urgent measures, or at least VND 20 million, where it is impossible to value such goods.
(b) A deed of guarantee issued by a bank or other credit institution.

126. When the lawsuit is brought, the court[18] shall issue a decision cancelling provisional urgent measures previously applied if either the defendant pays a counter-guarantee to release the measure[19] or the person subject to such measures proves that such application was not well-founded. When a provisional urgent measure is cancelled, the court shall consider refunding the applicant the security stipulated above. Where a request for the application of a provisional urgent measure was not well-founded, thus causing loss to the person subject to such measure, the court shall compel the applicant to pay compensation for such loss.

18. The authority and procedures for application of provisional urgent measures are implemented in accordance with the provisions of Chapter VIII, Part One of the Civil Procedure Code.
19. Clause 1 of Art. 122 of the Civil Procedure Code.

VII. Administrative Penalties

127. The following acts of infringement of industrial property rights are subject to administrative penalties:

(a) Acts of infringement of intellectual property rights which cause loss and damage to consumers or society.
(b) Failure to terminate an act of infringement of intellectual property rights although the intellectual property right holder has issued a written notice requesting termination of such act.[20]

Any person who commits an act of infringement of intellectual property rights is compelled to terminate such act and is subject to a caution or a monetary fine. In addition, depending on the nature and seriousness of the infringement, they may also be subject to one of the following additional penalties:

(a) Confiscation of intellectual property counterfeit goods, raw materials and materials, and facilities used mainly for production or trading of such intellectual property counterfeit goods.
(b) Suspension of business activities for a fixed period in the sector in which the infringement was committed.[21]

128. In addition to these penalties, any person who infringes intellectual property rights may also be subject to one or more of the following remedies:

(a) Compulsory destruction, distribution or use for non-commercial purposes of intellectual property counterfeit goods as well as raw materials, materials and facilities used mainly for production or trading of such intellectual property counterfeit goods, provided that such destruction, distribution or use will not affect the exploitation of rights by intellectual property rightholders.
(b) Compulsory transportation out of the territory of Vietnam of transit goods infringing intellectual property rights or compulsory re-export of intellectual property counterfeit goods and imported materials and raw materials, and facilities used mainly for production or trading of such intellectual property counterfeit goods after the infringing elements have been removed from such goods.

The minimum amount of the monetary fine is the value of the detected infringing goods, and the maximum amount shall not exceed five times such value.

20. Article 213 IPL.
21. Article 214 IPL.

§10. Overlapping and Relation to Other Intellectual Property Laws

129. Patent law does not overlap with other IPLs. However, the principles and rules of protection set forth for patents also apply to other industrial properties, particularly utility model patents, industrial design patents and layout designs. Moreover, the enforcement rules apply equally to all types of intellectual properties, such as copyright and trademark.

§11. Industrial Property Agents (Patent Agent)

I. Rights and Obligations of Industrial Property Agents

130. Industrial property representation service organizations (similar concept to patent agents in other countries) are organizations granted IP agent licences by NOIP to provide intellectual property-related services to customers. They shall only provide services within the scope of their authorization and may re-authorize other industrial property representation service organizations when they obtain written consent from the authorizing parties. Industrial property representation service organizations may voluntarily terminate their industrial property representation service business after having lawfully transferred all incomplete representation jobs to other industrial property representation service organizations.

131. Industrial property representatives must not perform the following activities:

(a) Concurrently represent different parties in dispute over industrial property rights.
(b) Withdraw applications for protection titles, declare waiver of protection or withdraw appeals against the establishment of industrial property rights without consent from the authorizing parties.
(c) Deceive their clients regarding contracts for industrial property representation services or force their clients to enter into and perform such contracts.

132. Industrial property representatives have the following responsibilities:

(a) To clearly notify their clients of fee and charge amounts and rates related to procedures for the establishment and protection of industrial property rights.
(b) To keep confidential information and documents related to cases in which they act as representatives.
(c) To truthfully and fully inform represented parties of all notices and requests from the State body competent to establish and protect industrial property rights; to deliver on time to the represented parties protection titles and other decisions.
(d) To promptly execute all requests regarding represented parties from the State body responsible for establishing and protecting industrial property rights to protect the legitimate rights and interests of the represented party.

(e) To notify the State body responsible for establishing and protecting industrial property rights of all changes in the names, addresses and other information of the represented parties when necessary.

Industrial property representation service organizations are civilly liable to the represented parties for representation performed by industrial property agents on behalf of such service organizations.

II. Conditions Applicable to Industrial Property Representation Service Business

133. Enterprises, cooperatives, law-practising organizations, and scientific and technological service organizations established and operating in accordance with the law have at least one individual with a representative service practise certificate. Industrial property owners are allowed to do business in industrial property representation services in the name of industrial property representation service organizations. Foreign law-practising organizations practising in Vietnam are not allowed to provide industrial property representation services.[22]

134. An individual who satisfies the following conditions is permitted to practice industrial property representation service:

(a) Has an industrial property representation service practising certificate.
(b) Works for an industrial property representation service organization.

Any individual who satisfies the following conditions is granted an industrial property representation service practising certificate:

(a) Is a Vietnamese citizen with full capacity for civil acts.
(b) Resides permanently in Vietnam.
(c) Has a bachelor's degree or equivalent diploma in case of practising in the field of trademarks, geographical indications, trade names, anti-unfair competition, and business secrets; Have a bachelor's degree or equivalent degree in natural sciences or technical sciences in case of practising in the fields of inventions, industrial designs, and layout designs.
(d) Has been engaged personally in the area of industrial property law for five consecutive years or more, or in the examination of assorted industrial property registration applications at national or international industrial property offices for five consecutive years or more, or has graduated from a training course on industrial property law recognized by the competent body.
(e) Is not a civil servant or employee working in the State body competent to establish and enforce industrial property rights.

22. Article 154 IPL.

(f) Has passed an examination on the industrial property representation profession organized by the competent body.

135. Licensed lawyers who are permanently residing in Vietnam will be exempted from obtaining an industrial property representation service practising certificate and will granted a Certificate to practice industrial property representation services in the fields of trademarks, geographical indications, trade names, anti-unfair competition, and business secrets if they graduated from an industrial property law training course recognized by NOIP.

136. The NOIP provides detailed programmes on industrial property law training and examinations for the industrial property representation profession, as well as on the grant of industrial property representation service practising certificates.

Where there are grounds to confirm that an industrial property representative no longer satisfies the business or practising conditions, NOIP shall delete the name of such industrial property representative from the National Register of Industrial Property and publish such deletion in the Official Gazette of Industrial Property.

Industrial property agents who make professional mistakes while practising shall, depending on the nature and seriousness of their mistake or breach, be subject to a warning, monetary fine or withdrawal of their industrial property representation service practising certificate.

Chapter 3. Utility Models

§1. Sources: Legislation

137. Utility models (or utility solutions) are subject to the same patent regulations, except that the definition of utility model does not require an inventive step. Accordingly, an invention, which is not too obvious as common knowledge, can have protection in the form of the grant of a utility model patent when it satisfies the following conditions: novelty and susceptibility of industrial application. Since the requirements for utility models are more relaxed than those for patents, it gives Vietnam, with its low level of technology, an opportunity to protect its innovative solutions. The following table shows this trend:

Applications for the Protection of Utility Models Filed from 1989–2021

Year	*Applications for Utility Model Filed By*		
	Vietnamese	*Foreigners*	*Total*
1989	25	–	25
1990	39	25	64
1991	52	01	53
1992	32	01	33
1993	38	20	58
1994	34	24	58
1995	26	39	65
1996	41	38	79
1997	24	42	66
1998	15	13	28
1999	28	14	42
2000	35	58	93
2001	35	47	82
2002	67	64	131
2003	76	51	127
2004	103	62	165
2005	182	66	248
2006	160	76	236
2007	120	100	220
2008	116	168	284
2009	133	120	253
2010	215	84	299
2011	193	114	307

Applications for the Protection of Utility Models Filed from 1989–2021

Year	*Applications for Utility Model Filed By*		
	Vietnamese	*Foreigners*	*Total*
2012	198	100	298
2013	227	104	331
2014	246	127	373
2015	310	140	450
2016	326	152	478
2017	273	161	434
2018	370	187	557
2019	395	204	599
2020	485	189	674
2021	449	146	595
Total	5,068	2,737	7,805

Source: NOIP.

Likewise, the chance of acceptance of an application for a utility models patent is also higher than that for a patent. The following table shows this assessment:

Granted Protection Titles for Utility Models from 1990–2021

Year	*Protection Titles for Utility Models Granted To*		
	Vietnamese	*Foreigners*	*Total*
1990	23		23
1991	44	1	45
1992	23	1	24
1993	9	1	10
1994	18	9	27
1995	8	16	24
1996	5	6	11
1997	8	12	20
1998	3	14	17
1999	6	12	18
2000	10	13	23
2001	17	9	26
2002	21	26	47
2003	28	27	55

Granted Protection Titles for Utility Models from 1990–2021			
Year	*Protection Titles for Utility Models Granted To*		
	Vietnamese	*Foreigners*	*Total*
2004	44	25	69
2005	41	33	74
2006	45	25	70
2007	49	36	85
2008	48	27	75
2009	45	19	64
2010	35	23	58
2011	46	23	69
2012	59	28	87
2013	74	33	107
2014	66	20	86
2015	86	31	117
2016	114	24	138
2017	118	28	146
2018	290	65	355
2019	230	72	302
2020	201	77	278
2021	187	63	250
Total	2,001	799	2,800

Source: NOIP.

The trend also shows that, since 2012, the number of utility models granted protection has not significantly increased.

§2. The Protection of Utility Models

138. A utility model patent is valid from the grant date until the end of ten years after the filing date. Apart from that, all other regulations for patents also apply to utility models.

Chapter 4. Trademarks

§1. Sources: Legislation

139. Trademark protection is provided under Chapter III of the IPL. IPL procedure for trademark registration is the same as the procedure for patent registration, except for some provisions to be provided below. Trademark infringement, particularly counterfeit goods, is the most popular form of infringement in Vietnam and is therefore subject to special attention, including detention of suspect goods by customs, as well as destruction of counterfeit goods. Trademark registration has become a familiar concept for Vietnamese businesses. The following table shows the statistics on registration of trademarks in Vietnam since 1982:

Certificates for Trademarks Granted from 1982–2021

Year	*Certificates for Trademarks Granted To*		
	Vietnamese	*Foreigners*	*Total*
1982–1989	380	1,170	1,550
1990	423	265	688
1991	1,525	388	1,913
1992	1,487	1,821	3,308
1993	1,395	2,137	3,532
1994	1,744	2,342	4,086
1995	1,627	2,965	4,592
1996	1,383	2,548	3,931
1997	980	1,506	2,486
1998	1,095	2,016	3,111
1999	1,299	2,499	3,798
2000	1,423	1,453	2,876
2001	2,085	1,554	3,639
2002	3,386	1,814	5,200
2003	4,907	2,243	7,150
2004	5,444	2,156	7,600
2005	6,427	3,333	9,760
2006	6,335	2,505	8,840
2007	10,660	5,200	15,860
2008	15,826	7,464	23,290
2009	16,231	6,499	22,730
2010	12,313	4,207	16,520
2011	15,502	5,938	21,440

Certificates for Trademarks Granted from 1982–2021			
Year	*Certificates for Trademarks Granted To*		
	Vietnamese	*Foreigners*	*Total*
2012	14,976	5,066	20,042
2013	14,503	5,156	19,659
2014	15,378	5,201	20,579
2015	14,207	4,133	18,340
2016	13,672	4,368	18,040
2017	15,172	4,229	19,401
2018	14,492	4,070	18,562
2019	22,265	6,555	28,820
2020	25,659	8,041	33,700
2021	25,379	7,621	33,000
Total	289,582	118,464	408,046

Source: NOIP.

§2. Subject Matter of Protection

I. Signs Which May Serve as Trademarks

140. A mark is eligible for protection when it satisfies the following conditions:[23]

(1) it is a visible sign in the form of letters, words, drawings or images, including holograms, or a combination thereof, represented in one or more colours or audio signals expressed in graphic form; and
(2) it is capable of distinguishing goods or services of the mark owner from those of other subjects.

From the above definitions, the following signs are considered not distinguishable and, therefore, ineligible for protection as trademarks:[24]

(1) Signs identical with or confusingly similar to national flags or national emblems, national anthems of Vietnam and of other countries, international anthems.
(2) Signs identical with or confusingly similar to emblems, flags, armorial bearings, abbreviated names or full names of Vietnamese State bodies, political

23. Article 72 IPL.
24. Article 73 IPL.

organizations, socio-political organizations, socio-politico-professional organizations, social organizations or socio-professional organizations or with international organizations, unless permitted by such bodies or organizations.

(3) Signs identical with or confusingly similar to real names, aliases, pseudonyms or images of leaders, national heroes or famous personalities of Vietnam or foreign countries.

(4) Signs identical to or confusingly similar to certification seals, check seals or warranty seals of international organizations which require that their signs must not be used unless such seals are registered as certification marks by such organizations.

(5) Signs which cause misunderstanding or confusion or deceive consumers as to the origin, properties, use, quality, value or other characteristics of goods or services.

(6) A sign is the inherent shape of the goods or is required by the technical characteristics of the goods.

(7) Signs containing copies of works unless authorized by the owner of the work.

II. Different Categories of Marks

141. Although mark means any sign used to distinguish goods or services of different persons, there are certain categories of marks that may be subject to different regulations, as follows:

(1) Collective mark means a mark used to distinguish goods or services of members of an organization which is the owner of such mark from marks of non-members. For example, HCA is the collective mark of the members of the Ho Chi Minh City Computer Association.

(2) Certification mark means a mark which is authorized by its owner to be used by another person on the latter's goods or services in order to certify the origin, raw materials, materials, mode of manufacture of goods or manner of provision of services, and the quality, accuracy, safety or other characteristics of goods or services bearing such mark. For example, HANG VIET NAM CHAT LUONG CAO (Vietnam High-Quality Products) is the certification mark of Saigon Tiep Thi Newspaper to be given to the local high-quality goods, as voted by consumers every year.

(3) Integrated marks means identical or similar marks registered by the same entity and intended for use on products or services which are of the same, similar or interrelated type. For example, CAMRY, COROLLA, and VIOS are integrated marks of the TOYOTA car manufacturing company.

(4) Well-known mark means a mark widely known by consumers throughout the territory of Vietnam, such as PETROVIETNAM or HEINEKEN.

The following criteria are taken into account when considering whether or not a mark is well known:[25]

(1) The number of relevant consumers who were aware of the mark by purchase or use of goods or services bearing the mark or from advertising.
(2) The territorial area in which goods or services bearing the mark are circulated.
(3) Turnover of the sale of goods or provision of services bearing the mark or the quantity of goods sold or services provided.
(4) Duration of continuous use of the mark.
(5) Wide reputation of goods or services bearing the mark.
(6) Number of countries protecting the mark.
(7) Number of countries recognizing the mark as a well-known mark.
(8) Assignment price, licensing price, or investment capital contribution value of the mark.

§3. Conditions of Protection

142. As noted, to be protected as a trademark, a mark has to be distinctive. Under Article 74 IPL, distinctiveness of marks is categorized as follows:

(1) A mark is deemed distinctive if it consists of one or more easily noticeable and memorable elements or of many elements forming an easily noticeable and memorable combination, and it does not fall into the cases stipulated in clause (2) below.
(2) A mark is deemed indistinctive if it is a sign falling into one of the following categories:
   (a) Simple shapes and geometric figures, numerals, letters or scripts of uncommon languages, except where such sign has been widely used and recognized as a mark before the filling date.
   (b) Conventional signs or symbols, pictures or common names in any language of goods or services and the usual shape of the goods or part of the goods, the usual shape of the packaging or container of the goods that has been in regular use and widely recognized before the filing date.
   (c) Signs indicating time, place and method of production; category, quantity, quality, properties, ingredients, use, value or other characteristics descriptive of goods or services, or signs that add significant value to the goods, except where such sign has acquired distinctiveness by use before the filing date.
   (d) Signs describing the legal status and business sector of business entities.
   (e) Signs indicating the geographical origin of goods or services, except where such sign has been widely used and recognized as a mark before the filing date or registered as a collective mark or certification mark as stipulated in IPL.

25. Article 75 IPL.

(f) Signs which are identical with or confusingly similar to registered marks of identical or similar goods or services on the basis of applications for registration with earlier filing dates or priority dates, as applicable, including applications for registration of marks filed pursuant to a treaty of which the Socialist Republic of Vietnam is a member, unless the trademark registration is terminated or invalidated.

(g) Signs identical with or confusingly similar to another person's mark which has been widely used and recognized for similar or identical goods or services before the filing date or the priority date, as applicable.

(h) Signs identical with or confusingly similar to another person's mark which has been registered for identical or similar goods or services, the registration certificate of which has been invalidated for no more than three years, except where the ground for such invalidation was non-use of the mark (*see* paragraph 153 below, referred to sub-clause (d) of Article 95.1 IPL).

(i) Signs identical with or confusingly similar to another person's mark recognized as a well-known trademark before the filling date which has been registered for goods or services which are identical with or similar to those bearing such well-known mark, or for dissimilar goods or services if the use of such mark may affect the distinctiveness of the well-known mark or the mark registration was aimed at taking advantage of the reputation of the well-known mark.

(j) Signs identical with or similar to another person's trade name currently in use if the use of such sign may cause confusion to consumers as to the origin of goods or services.

(k) Signs identical with or similar to a protected geographical indication if the use of such sign may mislead consumers as to the geographical origin of goods.

(l) Signs identical with, containing or being translated or transcribed from protected geographical indications for wines or spirits if such sign has been registered for use with respect to wines and spirits not originating from the geographical areas bearing such geographical indications.

(m) Signs identical with or insignificantly different from another person's industrial design which has been protected on the basis of an application for registration of an industrial design with a filing date or priority date earlier than that of the application for registration of the mark.

(n) A sign that is identical or confusingly similar to a plant variety name that has been or is being protected in Vietnam if that sign is registered for goods that are plant varieties of the same or similar species or harvested products. from plant varieties;

(o) The sign is identical or confusingly similar to the name, image of a character or image in another person's work under the scope of copyright protection that was widely known before the filing date, except with the permission of the owner of that work

§4. Formalities (Procedure for Protection, Establishing and Maintaining Trademarks)

143. For trademarks (except well-known marks), industrial property rights are established on the basis of registration at NOIP. The time for examination and registration is approximately twelve to eighteen months from the filing. The procedure to grant trademarks is the same as the procedure to grant a patent (*see* Part I, Chapter 2, §4 above), subject to a number of variations. Each registration application may request the grant of one certificate of registered mark for one mark to be used for one or more different goods or services. In the case of a well-known mark, industrial property rights are established on the basis of use and shall not be dependent on registration procedures.

In addition to the declaration in the application, there are a number of documents, samples and information identifying a mark which need to be included in an application for registration of a mark. They also include:

(a) a sample of the mark and a list of goods or services bearing the mark;
(b) regulations on the use of collective marks or regulations on the use of certification marks.

The sample of the mark must be described in order to clarify elements of the mark and the comprehensive meaning of the mark, if any; where the mark consists of words or phrases of hieroglyphic languages, such words or phrases must be transcribed; where the mark consists of words or phrases in a foreign language, such words or phrases must be translated into Vietnamese.

144. Goods or services listed in an application for registration of a mark must be classified into appropriate groups in accordance with the Classification List under the Nice Agreement on International Classification of Goods and Services for the purpose of mark registration and published by NOIP.

The regulations on the use of collective marks shall contain the following principal contents:

(a) Name, address, grounds of establishment and operation of the collective organization which owns the mark.
(b) Criteria for becoming a member of the collective organization.
(c) List of rightholders permitted to use the mark.
(d) Conditions for use of the mark.
(e) Measures for dealing with breaches of regulations on the use of the mark.

The regulations on the use of certification marks shall contain the following principal contents:

(a) The person being the mark owner.
(b) Conditions for using the mark.
(c) Characteristics of goods or services certified by the mark.

(d) Methods of evaluating characteristics of goods or services and methods of controlling the use of the mark.
(e) Expenses to be paid by the mark user for certification and protection of the mark, if any.

Please note that for trademark registration, the examination period for an industrial design, a mark or a geographical indication is six months from the date of publication of the application at the Industrial Properties Official Gazette.[26]

§5. Ownership and Transfer (Assignment: Licences)

I. Right to Register Marks

145. Rightholders have the right to register marks to be used for goods such persons produce or for services such persons provide.[27] Any person lawfully engaged in commercial activities has the right to register a mark for a product which he puts onto the market but which was manufactured by others, provided that the manufacturer does not use such mark for a product and does not object to such registration.

146. As for collective marks, lawfully established collective organizations have the right to register collective marks to be used by the members of the collective organization pursuant to the regulations of the collective organization on the use of collective marks. For signs indicating the geographical origins of goods or services, an organization with the right to register means a local collective organization of other persons engaged in production or trading in the relevant locality.

As for certified marks, organizations with the function of controlling and certifying quality, properties, origin or other relevant criteria of goods or services have the right to register certification marks, provided that such organizations are not engaged in the production or trading of such goods or services.

147. Two or more persons have the right to jointly register a mark in order to become its co-owners on the following conditions:

(a) Such mark is used in the names of all co-owners or used for goods or services which are produced or traded with the participation of all co-owners.
(b) The use of such a mark does not cause confusion among consumers as to the origin of goods or services.

Persons with the registration right stipulated above, including those who have already filed registration applications, may assign the registration right to other persons by a written contract, bequest or inheritance, provided that the assignee satisfies the conditions applicable to persons with the registration right.

26. Article 119 IPL.
27. Article 87 IPL.

148. For a mark protected in a country which is a contracting party to a treaty of which the Socialist Republic of Vietnam is a member and where the treaty prohibits the representative or agent of a mark owner from registering such mark, the representative or agent shall not be permitted to register such mark without agreement from the mark owner unless there is a justifiable reason.

Owner of a mark means a person who is granted a protection title for such mark by the competent body or who has an internationally registered mark recognized by the competent body or who has a well-known mark.

Once granted, the trademark registration certificate is valid from the date of grant until the expiry of ten years from the date of application and is renewable. At least six months before the expiry date, the trademark owner must apply to renew the trademark and pay the fee accordingly. The trademark will be terminated if not renewed within six months of the expiry date.

II. Assignment of Trademark

149. A trademark can be assigned in the same manner as patents (*see* Chapter 2 §5 II above), provided that such assignment does not confuse the public, that is, both old and new owners can use the same trademark without a licensing relationship. That means the assignment of the rights to marks must not cause confusion as to the properties or origins of goods or services bearing such marks. Also, rights to marks may only be assigned to persons who have satisfied the conditions for a right to register. Last but not least, the right to use collective marks must not be licensed to persons other than members of the owners of such collective marks.

150. If the trademark owner would like to have more than one trademark user, he or she must sign a licence agreement. In case of trademark licence, mark licensees must indicate on the goods and their packages that such goods have been manufactured under mark licence contracts. The form, content and validity of the licence contract are governed in the same manner as patents. Please also note that the term of a trademark licence cannot be longer than the term of protection of the trademark itself, and therefore, continuation of the licence would require an extension of trademark by the trademark owner.

§6. Scope of Exclusive Rights

151. As with patents, a trademark owner has the exclusive right to use the trademark, to dispose of the trademark, and to prevent others from using the trademark without his consent (except when limited use is allowed). Use of a mark means the performance of the following acts:

(a) Affixing the protected mark on goods, goods packages, business facilities, means of service provision or transaction documents in business activities.

(b) Circulating, offering, advertising for sale or stocking for sale goods bearing the protected mark.
(c) Importing goods or services bearing the protected mark.

§7. Limitations of the Scope of Trademark Protection

152. The scope of trademark protection is similar to that of patent protection (*see* Chapter 2 §7 above). The difference is in cases of prior use. Instead of the concept of prior invention (*see* Chapter 2 §7 I above), IPL provides that the use of marks identical or similar to protected geographical indications without consent of the right holder of the geographical indication is allowed where such marks have acquired protection in an honest manner before the date of filing the application for registration of such geographical indication.

In addition, using people's names, descriptive marks of type, quantity, quality, utility, value, geographical origin and other properties of goods or services in an honest manner is also allowed without the consent of the trademark owner.

§8. Use Requirements

153. Owners of marks must use such marks continuously. Where a mark has not been used for five consecutive years or more, the ownership right to such mark is invalidated in accordance with the provisions of Article 95 of IPL.

§9. Duration of Protection: Renewal: Termination

154. A certificate of registered mark is valid from the grant date until the end of ten years after the filing date and may be renewed for multiple consecutive terms, each with a ten-year duration.

A trademark can be terminated for the following reasons:

(a) The mark has not been used by its owner or the licensee of the owner without justifiable reason for five consecutive years prior to a request for termination of validity, except where use is commenced or resumed at least three months before the request for termination.
(b) The owner of a certificate of registered collective mark fails to supervise or ineffectively supervises the implementation of the regulations on the use of the collective mark.
(c) The owner of a certificate of registered certification mark violates the regulations on the use of the certification mark or fails to supervise or ineffectively supervises the implementation of such regulations.

For marks, the petition for termination of trademark is subject to statute of limitation. Such statute of limitations is five years from the grant date, except where the protection title was granted as a result of the dishonesty of the applicant.

The provisions on trademark termination also apply to the termination of validity of international registrations of marks.

§10. Infringement and Remedies

I. Definition of Infringements, Measures Against Counterfeit Goods

155. Under Article 129 IPL, the following acts, if performed without the permission of mark owners, are deemed to be infringements of trademark rights:

(a) Using signs identical with protected marks for goods or services identical with goods or services on the list registered together with such mark.
(b) Using signs identical with protected marks for goods or services similar or related to those goods or services on the list registered together with such mark if such use is likely to cause confusion as to the origin of the goods or services.
(c) Using signs similar to protected marks for goods or services identical with, similar to or related to goods or services on the list registered together with such mark if such use is likely to cause confusion as to the origin of the goods or services.
(d) Using signs identical with, or similar to, well-known marks, or signs in the form of translations or transcriptions of well-known marks for any goods or services, including those not identical with, dissimilar or unrelated to goods or services on the lists of those bearing well-known marks, if such use is likely to cause confusion as to the origin of the goods or services or misleading impressions as to the relationship between users of such signs and well-known mark owners.

156. Provisions on trademark infringement and remedies are the same as those regarding patent infringement and remedies (*see* Chapter 2 §9 above). In addition, IPL provides extra protection against trademark violations regarding the act of producing, importing, transporting or trading in intellectual property counterfeit goods or assigning others to do so. Intellectual property counterfeit goods comprise goods bearing counterfeit marks and goods bearing counterfeit geographical indications (hereinafter referred to as counterfeit mark goods). Counterfeit mark goods are defined as goods or their packages bearing a mark or sign which is identical to or indistinguishable from a mark or geographical indication currently protected for those very goods without permission from the mark owner or organization managing the geographical indication.

157. Also, trademark infringement includes the act of producing, importing, transporting or trading in articles bearing a mark or geographical indication which is identical or confusingly similar to a protected mark or geographical indication or assigning others to do so.

Decree No. 99/2013/ND-CP of 29 August 2013, providing for sanction of Administrative Violations in the field of intellectual property, specifies the acts of infringement of intellectual property rights which are subject to administrative penalties, the forms and levels of penalties, and the procedures for applying such penalties. Any person who commits an act of unfair competition in intellectual property is subject to an administrative penalty in accordance with the law on competition.

II. Preventive Measures and/or Measures to Secure Enforcement of Administrative Penalties

158. Before the issuance of the Law on amendment to the IPL 2022, in case of trademark and industrial design violation, under Article 215 IPL, rightholders have the right to request the competent body to apply preventive measures and/or measures to secure enforcement of the administrative penalties when:

(a) An act of infringement of intellectual property rights is likely to cause serious loss and damage to consumers or society.
(b) Material evidence of the infringement is likely to be dispersed, or there are indications that the offender will evade responsibility.
(c) Necessary to secure enforcement of a decision imposing an administrative penalty.

Preventive measures and/or measures to secure enforcement of administrative penalties which may be applied in accordance with administrative procedures to acts of infringement of intellectual property rights, shall comprise:

(a) temporary detention of persons;
(b) temporary custody of infringing goods, material evidence and facilities;
(c) body searches;
(d) searches of means of transport and objects; searches of places where infringing goods, material evidence and facilities are hidden;
(e) other administrative preventive measures in accordance with the law on dealing with administrative breaches.

However, the Law on amendment to the IPL 2022 abolished Article 215 because the above measures were prescribed in the Law on Handling of Administrative Violations 2012.

III. Control of Intellectual Property Related Imports and Exports

A. *Border Control Measures*

159. In addition to other civil, criminal and administrative measures to handle intellectual property infringement, which have been outlined in the patent Chapter (*see* Chapter 2 §9 above), IPL also provides measures to control intellectual property-related imports and exports, which comprise:[28]

28. Article 216 IPL.

(a) suspension of customs procedures for goods suspected of infringing intellectual property rights;
(b) inspection and supervision to detect goods showing signs of infringing intellectual property rights.

Suspension of customs procedures for goods suspected of infringing intellectual property rights is a measure taken at the request of an intellectual property right holder in order to collect information and evidence on the goods consignment in question so that the intellectual property right holder may exercise the right to request that the infringing act be dealt with and to request the application of provisional urgent measures, preventive measures and/or measures to secure enforcement of administrative penalties. In addition, customs authorities are also obliged to proactively take action if during the process of inspection, supervision and control, they discover clear grounds to suspect that exported or imported goods are counterfeit goods.

160. Inspection and supervision to detect goods showing signs of infringing intellectual property rights is a measure taken at the request of an intellectual property right holder in order to collect information for the exercise of the right to request suspension of customs procedures.

If any intellectual property counterfeit goods are found during the course of the application of the suspension and inspection measures, the customs office has the responsibility to apply administrative remedies to deal with such goods in accordance with IPL.[29]

At the same time, the IPL also provides in Article 217 obligations of applicants for measures to control intellectual property-related imports and exports, as follows:

(a) To prove that the applicant is an intellectual property right holder by producing the documents and evidence stipulated in clause 2 of Article 203 of IPL.
(b) To supply information sufficient to identify goods suspected of infringing intellectual property rights or to detect goods showing signs of infringing intellectual property rights.
(c) To file a written request with the customs office and to pay the fees and charges stipulated by law.
(d) To pay damages and other expenses incurred to persons subject to control measures in a case where the controlled goods are found not to have infringed industrial property rights.

In order to secure the performance of the obligation stipulated in sub-paragraph (d) of clause 1 of this article, an applicant shall deposit security in one of the following forms:

29. Articles 214 and 215 of IPL.

(a) A sum of money equal to 20% of the value of the goods consignment subject to the application of the measure of suspension of customs procedures, or at least VND 20 million where it is impossible to value such goods.
(b) A deed of guarantee issued by a bank or other credit institution.[30]

IV. Procedures for Application of the Suspending Customs Procedures

161. When an applicant for the suspension of customs procedures has fulfilled the obligations mentioned in section A above, the customs office shall issue a decision suspending customs procedures with regard to the goods consignment in question. Customs authorities provide intellectual property rights holders with information about the name and address of the consignor; exporter, consignee or importer; goods description; quantity of goods; the country of origin of the goods, if known, within thirty days from the date of issuance of the decision to apply administrative measures to handle counterfeit trademark goods and illegally copied goods. The duration of suspension of customs procedures is ten working days from the date of issuance of the suspension decision. Where the applicant has justifiable reasons, this duration may be extended but must not exceed twenty working days.

Upon expiry of the ten or twenty-day period above, if the applicant does not initiate civil proceedings and the customs office does not issue a decision accepting jurisdiction to deal with the case in accordance with administrative procedures as an administrative breach by the importer or exporter of the goods, then the customs office has the following responsibilities:

(a) To continue customs procedures for the goods consignment in question.
(b) To compel the applicant to compensate for all loss and damage caused to the owner of the goods consignment due to the unreasonable request for suspension of customs procedures and to pay expenses for warehousing and preservation of goods, as well as other expenses incurred by the customs office and any related body or person, in accordance with the law on customs.
(c) To refund to the applicant the remaining security amount after the obligation to pay compensation and expenses stipulated in sub-paragraph (b) above has been fulfilled.

162. Where an intellectual property right holder requests inspection and supervision to detect goods showing signs of infringement of intellectual property rights and the customs office then finds such a goods consignment, the customs office shall promptly notify the applicant. If the applicant does not request the suspension of customs procedures with regard to the offending goods consignment and the customs office does not issue a decision on consideration of the application of the administrative penalties within three working days from the date of notification, then the customs office must continue carrying out customs procedures for the goods consignment in question.

30. *See* clause 2 of Art. 217 of IPL.

163. In case the customs authority proactively suspends customs procedures, the customs authority must immediately notify the intellectual property rights holder if there is contact information and the importer or exporter about the suspension.

164. Within ten working days from the date of notification, if the intellectual property rights holder does not initiate a civil lawsuit and the customs authority does not decide to accept the case according to the procedures for handling administrative violations, the customs authority will be responsible for continuing to carry out customs procedures for the goods consignment.

§11. Overlapping and Relation to Other Intellectual Property Laws

165. As noted in the chapter on copyright (*see* Chapter 1 §11 above), there are overlaps between the protection of trademark, copyright, and even industrial design. However, each of the rights protects a different aspect of creativity. In case there is an overlap between trademark and copyright, the trademark right usually prevails because trademark is an exclusive right to use a symbol and to prevent others from using that symbol (regardless of whether the use was a copy or not), whereas copyright is only a right to prevent the copy of a work. In the meantime, when there is an overlap between trademark and industrial design, the question is whether these two certificates of protection (trademark and industrial design) cover the same scope of protection. When the answer is affirmative, the question is then who filed for registration first. The certificate holder who filed later and knew about the registration of the other is deemed to have violated the rights of the first to file.

Chapter 5. Trade Names

§1. Sources: Legislation

166. Trade name means the designation of an organization or individual used in business activities in order to distinguish the business entity bearing such trade name from other business entities in the same business sector and area.[31] 'Business area' means the geographical area in which a business entity has its partners, customers or reputation.

Compared to trademark, trade name or trade dress comes into the scope of protection later (until Decree 54/2000/ND-CP, as a result of Vietnam entering into the Vietnam US Bilateral Trade Agreement). Trade name protection is provided in Chapter III of IPL, in the same section as trademark. Industrial property rights to a trade name are established on the basis of lawful use of the name. It is not required to register at NOIP in order to be protected, and registration is generally considered a backup solution when a claim for trademark infringement is not successful, either because the marks are not confusingly similar or because the legitimate user of the trademark has not yet registered its trademark at NOIP. Like trade name, protection against unfair competition also serves as a 'safety net'. Both are presented in this chapter.

§2. The Protection of Trade Names

167. Under Article 76 IPL, a trade name is protected when it is capable of distinguishing the business entity bearing it from other business entities operating in the same business sector and locality. However, there are certain objects ineligible for protection as trade names, such as names of State bodies, political organizations, socio-political organizations, socio-politico-professional organizations, social organizations, socio-professional organizations and other entities not involved in business activities.

A trade name is deemed to be distinctive when it satisfies the following conditions:

(1) It consists of a proper name, except where the proper name was widely known by use.
(2) It is not identical with or confusingly similar to a trade name which was used earlier by another person in the same business sector and locality.
(3) It is not identical with or confusingly similar to another person's mark or a geographical indication which was protected before the date of use of such trade name.[32]

31. Article 4.21 IPL.
32. Article 78 IPL.

168. Owner of a trade name means a person (legal or physical entity) who lawfully uses such trade name in business activities. The owner of the trade name bears the onus of proof that he is the trade name user before the court when filing a claim alleging trade name violation.

Use of a trade name means the performance of acts for commercial purposes by using the trade name to name oneself in business activities or expressing the trade name in or on transaction documents, signboards, products, goods, goods packages and means of service provision or advertisement.

Rights to trade names may only be assigned together with the transfer of the entire business establishment and business activities under such trade name.

Although IPL protects trade names, using people's names or descriptive types of quantity in an honest manner would be allowed without the consent of the trade name owner.

Infringement of trade name means the act of using commercial indications identical with, or similar to, trade names of others which were used earlier for the same or similar type of goods or services and which cause confusion as to business entities, establishments or activities under such trade names.

§3. Acts of Unfair Competition

169. The right to prevent unfair competition is established on the basis of competitive activities in business. The following acts are deemed to be acts of unfair competition:

(a) Using commercial indications to cause confusion as to business entities, business activities or commercial origin of goods or services.
(b) Using commercial indications to cause confusion as to the origin, production method, utilities, quality, quantity or other characteristics of goods or services; or as to the conditions for the provision of goods or services.
(c) Using marks protected in a country which is a contracting party to a treaty of which the Socialist Republic of Vietnam is a member and under which representatives or agents of owners of such marks are prohibited from using such marks if users are representatives or agents of the mark owners and such use is neither consented to by the mark owners nor justified.
(d) Possessing or using domain names identical with, or confusingly similar to, protected trade names or marks of others, or geographical indications without having the right to use, with bad faith, benefiting from the reputation and popularity of the respective mark, trade name or geographical indication to gain illegal profits.

170. Commercial indications mean signs and information serving as guidelines for trading of goods or services, including marks, trade names, business symbols, business slogans, geographical indications, designs of packages and/or labels of goods. Acts of using commercial indications include acts of affixing such commercial indications on goods, goods packages, means of service provision, business transaction documents or advertisements; and selling, advertising for sale, stocking for sale and importing goods affixed with such commercial indications.

Chapter 6. Industrial Designs

§1. Sources: Legislation

171. Industrial design means the outward appearance of a product embodied in three-dimensional configuration, lines, colours or a combination of such elements.[33] Regulations on industrial designs are provided in Chapter III (industrial property rights). As such, most of the regulations on patents can also be applied with respect to industrial designs, except for certain regulations pertaining to the industrial application and the role of the use of patents for public interest. Compared to patents, it is much less likely to be held that a design owner has to use an industrial design according to the public need. This is because the design pertains to the aesthetic aspects of the good rather than the function or usage of it.

172. More Vietnamese enterprises register industrial designs than foreign enterprises. The largest registered category of design is label. This is also because the regulations on design registration are more relaxed than trademark registration regulations, and therefore to some extent enterprises may register a label in lieu of a trademark registration. The following table describes the design registration situation in Vietnam:

Granted Protection Titles for Industrial Designs from 1989–2021

Year	*Protection Titles for Industrial Design Granted To*		
	Vietnamese	*Foreigners*	*Total*
1989	14	–	14
1990	91	9	100
1991	219	5	224
1992	433	6	439
1993	528	21	549
1994	524	27	551
1995	626	85	711
1996	798	68	866
1997	261	62	323
1998	728	94	822
1999	841	94	935
2000	526	119	645
2001	333	43	376
2002	368	9	377
2003	359	109	468

33. Article 4.13 IPL.

Granted Protection Titles for Industrial Designs from 1989–2021

Year	*Protection Titles for Industrial Design Granted To*		
	Vietnamese	*Foreigners*	*Total*
2004	412	235	647
2005	508	218	726
2006	678	497	1,175
2007	896	474	1,370
2008	908	429	1,337
2009	747	489	1,236
2010	832	320	1,152
2011	807	338	1,145
2012	681	440	1,121
2013	852	510	1,362
2014	984	650	1,634
2015	841	545	1,386
2016	877	577	1,454
2017	1,339	928	2,267
2018	1,083	1,277	2,360
2019	1,234	983	2,217
2020	1,110	956	2,066
2021	1,196	907	2,103
Total	2,2634	1,1524	3,4158

Source: NOIP.

§2. SUBJECT MATTER OF PROTECTION

173. An industrial design is eligible for protection when it satisfies the following conditions:

(a) It is novel.
(b) It is of a creative nature.
(c) It is susceptible to industrial application.[34]

From the above definition, the following items are ineligible for protection as industrial designs:

34. Article 63 IPL.

(1) Outward appearance of a product which is necessary due to the technical features of the product.
(2) Outward appearance of civil or industrial construction works.
(3) Shape of a product which is invisible during the use of the product.[35]

§3. Conditions of Protection

I. Novelty of Industrial Designs

174. An industrial design is deemed to be new if it significantly differs from other industrial designs which have been publicly disclosed by use or by means of written descriptions or in any other form either inside or outside Vietnam prior to the filing date or the priority date, as applicable, of the application for registration of the industrial design.

Two industrial designs shall not be deemed to be significantly different from each other if they are only different in features of appearance which are not easily noticeable and memorable and which cannot be used to distinguish such industrial designs overall. An industrial design is not deemed publicly disclosed if it is known to only a limited number of persons who must keep it secret.

175. Like patents (but with a shorter time limit), an industrial design is deemed not to have lost its novelty if published in the following cases, provided that the application for registration of the industrial design is filed within six months from the date of publication:

(a) It is published by another person without permission from the person having the right to register it.[36]
(b) It is published in the form of a scientific presentation by the person having the right to register it.
(c) It is displayed at a national exhibition of Vietnam or at an official or officially recognized international exhibition by the person having the right to register it.

II. Creativity of Industrial Designs

176. Under Article 66 IPL, an industrial design is deemed to be creative if it cannot be easily created by a person with average knowledge of the art, based on industrial designs already publicly disclosed through use, by means of written descriptions or by any other form either inside or outside of Vietnam. This assessment is made before the filing date or the priority date, as applicable, of the application for registration of the industrial design.

---

35. Article 64 IPL.
36. Defined in Art. 86 of IPL.

III. Susceptible of Industrial Application

177. An industrial design is deemed to be susceptible to industrial application if it can be used as a model for mass manufacture of products with the outward appearance embodying such industrial design by industrial or handicraft methods.

§4. Formalities (Procedure for Grant and Obtaining Protection)

178. The procedure for granting a protection title for an industrial design is similar to that for patents, with a few exceptions. Each registration application may request the grant of one industrial design patent for several industrial designs in the following cases:

(a) Industrial designs of a set of products consisting of numerous items expressing a single common inventive idea and used together or for a common purpose.
(b) An industrial design accompanied by one or more variants of such industrial design which express a single common inventive idea and are not significantly different from such industrial design.

Documents identifying an industrial design which needs to be protected in an application for registration of an industrial design shall include a description and a set of photos or drawings of such industrial design. The industrial design description shall consist of a descriptive section and a section on the scope of protection of such industrial design.

179. Like patents (*see* Chapter 2 §4 III above), the descriptive section of an industrial design must satisfy the following conditions:

(a) Fully disclose all features expressing the nature of the industrial design and clearly identify features which are new or different from the most similar known industrial design, and consistent with the set of photos or drawings.
(b) Where the application for registration of the industrial design consists of variants, the descriptive section must fully show these variants and clearly identify distinctions between the principal variant and other variants.
(c) Where the industrial design stated in the registration application is that of a set of products, the descriptive section must fully show the features of each product of the set.

180. The section on the scope of protection of an industrial design must clearly define features which need to be protected, including features which are new and different from similar known industrial designs. In addition, the set of photos and drawings must fully define the features of the industrial design. Applications for registration of industrial designs (same for marks or geographical indications) are published within two months from the date such application is accepted as being valid.

§5. Ownership and Transfer (Assignment: Licences)

181. The rights to register inventions shall belong to authors who have created industrial designs by their own labour and at their own expense or people who have supplied funds and material facilities to authors in the form of job assignment or hiring unless otherwise agreed by the parties involved. A person who has the registration right as stipulated in this article may assign such right to other persons by a written contract, bequest or inheritance, even where a registration application has already been filed.

182. In case the industrial designs are created by using material and technical facilities and funds from the State Budget, then the State shall have the right to register such industrial designs, or become the co-owner of the patents of such industrial designs, if they are created partly from the State Budget. Where a number of rightholders have jointly created or invested in the creation of an industrial design, such rightholders shall all have the registration right, which may only be exercised with the consensus of all. The eligible applicants, once granted the design patent, shall become the design owners. However, the law also provides protection to the authors, that is, those who have personally created the design. Where two or more persons have jointly created an industrial property object, they are co-authors of it. These authors shall enjoy the moral rights to be named as authors in the design patents and to be acknowledged as authors in documents in which designs are published or introduced. Moreover, authors shall also enjoy economic rights to receive remuneration.

§6. Scope of Exclusive Rights

183. As with patents, the design owner has the exclusive right to use the design, to transfer the design, and to prevent others from using the design without consent (except when limited use is allowed). Use of an industrial design means the performance of the following acts:

(a) Manufacturing products with an appearance embodying the protected industrial design.
(b) Circulating, advertising, offering or stocking for circulation products protected by a design patent.
(c) Importing products protected by design patent.

§7. Limitations of the Scope of Protection

184. The limitations of the scope of protection of industrial designs are the same as for patents (*see* Chapter 2 §7 above), except that the provisions on compulsory licensing shall not apply to industrial designs.

§8. Duration of Protection

185. An industrial design patent is valid from the grant date until the end of five years after the filing date and may be renewed for two consecutive terms, each of five years.

§9. Infringement and Remedies

186. The infringement and remedies for protection of industrial designs are the same as those for patents (*see* Chapter 2 §9 above) and trademarks (*see* Chapter 4 §10 above).

§10. Overlapping and Relation to Other Intellectual Property Laws

187. As noted in the chapters on copyright and trademark, there are overlaps between the protection of trademarks, copyrights, and even industrial designs. However, each of the rights protects a different aspect of creativity. In case there is an overlap between an industrial design and copyright, the industrial design right usually prevails because industrial design is an exclusive right to use a design and prevent others from using that design (regardless of whether the use was a copy or not), whereas copyright is only a right to prevent the copy of a work. In the meantime, when there is an overlap between trademarks and industrial designs, the question is whether these two certificates of protection (trademark and industrial design) cover the same scope of protection. When the answer is affirmative, the question is then who filed for registration first. The one who filed later and knew about the registration of the other is deemed to have violated the rights of the one who was first to file.

Chapter 7. Plant Variety Protection

§1. Sources: Legislation

188. Plant variety means a plant grouping within a single botanical taxation of the lowest known rank, which is morphologically uniform and suitable for being propagated unchanged and can be both defined by the expression of phenotypes resulting from a genotype or a combination of given genotypes and distinguished from any other plant grouping by the expression of at least one inheritable phenotype.[37]

189. Regulations on plant variety protection in Vietnam are still new, with their history dating back to 2004, not long after Vietnam entered into a Vietnam-US Bilateral Trade Agreement. These regulations are under the administration of the Ministry of Agriculture and Rural Development rather than the Ministry of Science and Technology (and the NOIP under it). Rights to a plant variety shall be established on the basis of a decision by the competent State body to grant a plant variety protection title in accordance with the registration procedures stipulated in Chapter IV of IPL. There are still no statistics on plant variety protection in Vietnam.

§2. Subject Matter of Protection

190. Plant varieties eligible for protection are plant varieties which have been selected and bred or discovered and developed, are on the list of State protected plant species promulgated by the Ministry of Agriculture and Rural Development, and are new, distinct, uniform, stable and designated by proper denominations.[38]

§3. Conditions of Protection

I. Novelty of a Plant Variety

191. A plant variety is deemed new if reproductive or harvested materials of this variety have not yet been sold or otherwise distributed for the purpose of exploitation in the territory of Vietnam by the registration right holder or his or her licensee one year before the filing date of the application for registration. For exploitation outside the territory of Vietnam, the applicable time period is six years before the filing date of the application for registration for timber trees or woody climbing plants or four years for other plant varieties.[39]

---

37. Article 4.24 IPL.
38. Article 158 IPL.
39. Article 159 IPL.

II. Distinctness of a Plant Variety

192. A plant variety is deemed distinct if it is clearly distinguishable from any other variety whose existence is a matter of common knowledge at the time of filing the application or on the priority date.

Plant varieties whose existence is a matter of common knowledge defined in clause 1 of this article are those falling into one of the following cases:

(a) Their reproductive materials or harvested materials have been widely used in the market of any country at the time of filing of the application for registration for protection.
(b) They have been protected or registered on the list of plant species in any country.
(c) They are the subject matter of an application for registration for protection or registration on the list of plant species in any country, provided that such application has not been rejected.
(d) Their detailed description has been published.[40]

III. Uniformity of a Plant Variety

193. A plant variety is deemed uniform if, subject to variation which may be expected from the particular features of its propagation, it is sufficiently uniform in its relevant characteristics.[41]

IV. Stability of a Plant Variety

194. A plant variety is deemed stable if its relevant originally described characteristics remain unchanged after repeated propagation or, in the case of a particular cycle of propagation, at the end of each cycle.[42]

V. Denominations of Plant Varieties

195. The registrant must designate a proper denomination for a plant variety which must match the denomination registered in any member country of the International Association for the Protection of New Plant Varieties and the country where an application for registration for protection was filed.[43]

40. Article 160 IPL.
41. Article 161 IPL.
42. Article 162 IPL.
43. Article 163 IPL.

The denomination of a plant variety is deemed proper if it is distinguishable from those of other plant varieties of common knowledge within the same or similar species. Likewise, denominations of plant varieties are deemed improper in the following cases:

(a) They consist of numerals only, except where such numerals are relevant to the characteristics or the breeding of such variety or include the species name of that plant variety.
(b) They violate social ethics.
(c) They may easily mislead as to features or characteristics or value of such variety.
(d) They may easily mislead as to the identification of the breeder.
(e) They are identical or confusingly similar to marks, trade names or geographical indications protected before the date of publication of the application for registration for protection of such plant variety.
(f) They are identical or similar to the denomination of a harvested material of such plant variety.
(g) They affect prior rights of other persons.

196. Rightholders who offer for sale or bring onto the market reproductive materials of plant varieties must use the denominations of such plant varieties as stated in protection titles even after the expiration of the protection terms.

When denominations of plant varieties are combined with marks, trade names or indications similar to denominations of plant varieties already registered for offer for sale or brought onto the market, such denominations must still be distinguishable.

In case the name of a plant variety registered for protection does not comply with the above requirements, the state management agency in charge of rights to plant varieties rejects that name and requires the registrant to propose another name within a time limit of thirty days from the date of issuance of the notice. The state management agency for plant variety rights records the official name of the plant variety from the time of granting the plant variety protection certificate.

§4. Formalities (Procedure for Grant and Obtaining Protection)

197. Rights to a plant variety are established on the basis of a decision of the competent State body to grant a plant variety protection title in accordance with the registration procedures stipulated in IPL.

I. Method of Filing Applications for Registration of Rights to Plant Varieties

198. Under Article 165 IPL, any Vietnamese person or any foreign person with a permanent residential address in Vietnam or who has a plant variety production or trading establishment in Vietnam may file an application for registration of rights to a plant variety (hereinafter referred to as protection registration application) either directly or by a lawful representative in Vietnam. In addition, any foreign person without a permanent residential address in Vietnam or without a plant variety production or trading establishment in Vietnam may file an application for registration of rights to a plant variety by a lawful representative in Vietnam.

199. Vietnam applies the 'first to file' principle to plant varieties. This means that when two or more parties independently file applications for registration for protection on different days for the same plant variety, a plant variety protection certificate shall only be granted to the earliest valid registrant. Where there are a number of applications for registration for protection of the same plant variety filed on the same day, a plant variety protection certificate shall only be granted to the registrant whose name is used for the filing of the sole application as agreed upon by all the other registrants. Where these registrants fail to reach an agreement, the State administrative body for rights to plant varieties shall consider granting a plant variety protection certificate to the party deemed to be the first breeder who selected and bred or discovered and developed such variety.

II. Priority Principle Applicable to Protection Registration Applications

200. A registrant may claim priority right when an application for registration for protection is filed within twelve months from the date of filing an application for registration for protection for the same plant variety in a country which has concluded an agreement on plant variety protection with Vietnam. The date on which the first filing occurred shall not be included in this time limit. In order to enjoy priority right, the registrant must express the claim for the priority right in his or her application for registration for protection. Within three months after filing the application, the registrant must produce copies of documents from the first application certified by the competent body and samples or other evidence proving that the variety in both applications was the same. The registrant must also pay a fee. The registrant may supply necessary information, documents or materials to the State administrative body for rights to plant varieties for examination within two years of expiry of the duration for enjoying the priority right, or within an appropriate duration depending on the species of the plant variety stated in the application after a first application is rejected or withdrawn. When an application for registration for protection is eligible for priority right, the priority date is the first filing date. The filing of another application or the publication or use of the plant variety which is the subject matter of the first application for registration for protection, shall not be deemed grounds for rejecting the application for registration for protection eligible for the priority right.

III. Plant Variety Protection Certificates: National Register of Protected Plant Varieties

201. A protection certificate for a plant variety shall state the denomination and species of such variety, the name of the owner of rights to such plant variety (hereinafter referred to as the protection certificate holder), the name of the plant variety breeder and the duration of the term of protection of rights to the plant variety. The State administrative body for rights to plant varieties shall record the grant and contents of a protection certificate in the National Register of Protected Plant Varieties. It also archives such information.

202. A protection certificate holder may request the State administrative body for rights to plant varieties to amend or correct errors related to the name and address of the holder on payment of fees and charges. Where such errors were made by the State administrative body for rights to plant varieties, such body must correct such errors, and protection certificate holders shall not have to pay fees and charges.

A protection certificate holder may request the State administrative body for rights to plant varieties to re-grant a plant variety protection certificate when such certificate was lost or damaged, provided that the holder pays fees and charges.

Decisions on the grant, re-grant, suspension, cancellation, and amendment of plant variety protection certificates are published by the State administrative body for rights to plant varieties in a specialized magazine on plant varieties within sixty days after such decisions are issued.

IV. Applications for Registration for Protection

203. An application for registration for protection (of a plant variety) shall contain the following documents:

(a) A declaration for registration made on the stipulated sample form.
(b) Photos and a technical declaration made on the stipulated sample form.
(c) Power of attorney, where the application is filed through a representative.
(d) Documents evidencing the registration right where the registrant is a transferee of the registration right.
(e) Documents evidencing the priority right where the application contains a claim for the priority right.
(f) Receipt for payment of fees and charges.

204. Applications for registration for protection and source documents of transactions between an applicant for registration and the State administrative body for rights to plant varieties are made in Vietnamese, except for the following documents which may be made in another language but shall be translated into Vietnamese at the request of the State administrative body for rights to plant varieties:

(a) Power of attorney.
(b) Documents evidencing the registration right.

(c) Documents evidencing the priority right.
(d) Other documents supporting the application (if applicable).[44]

205. Documents evidencing the priority right of an application for registration for protection of rights to a plant variety shall comprise (each application is registered only for the protection of one plant variety):

(a) copies of the first application(s) certified by the receiving agency;
(b) documents on transfer or inheritance of the priority right if such right is acquired from another person.

An application for registration for protection is considered received by the relevant State administrative body for rights to plant varieties only when the application contains all the documents stipulated above. The filing date of an application is the date on which such application is received by the relevant State administrative body for rights to plant varieties.

V. Formal Examination of Applications for Registration for Protection

206. The State administrative body for rights to plant varieties shall conduct a formal examination of an application within fifteen days of receipt of such application in order to determine the validity of such application. An application for registration for protection is deemed invalid in the following cases:

(a) It fails to satisfy the formal requirements as stipulated.
(b) The application is filed by a person who does not have the registration right, including where the registration right belongs to many persons, but one or more of them do not agree to register.

In the cases above, the State administrative body for rights to plant varieties shall carry out the following procedures:

(a) Notify the registrant of refusal to accept the application, clearly stating the reasons for refusal.
(b) Notify the registrant of errors for correction, setting a time limit of thirty days after the receipt of the notice for the correction of such errors by the registrant.
(c) Notify the registrant of refusal to accept the application where the registrant fails to correct errors or does not make a reasonable appeal against the notice above.
(d) Notify the registrant of the acceptance of the application where such application is valid or where the registrant has properly corrected the errors or made a justifiable opposition to the notice above, in which the State administrative body shall request for the supply samples of the plant variety to the testing institution for performance of technical tests and procedures within thirty days before the

44. Article 174 of IPL.

first planting season from the date of issuance of the notice of acceptance of the application for registration of protection of that plant variety, except in the case of plant varieties tested by the registrant himself.

207. Where an application is accepted as valid, the State administrative body for rights to plant varieties shall publish such valid application in a specialized magazine on plant varieties within ninety days from the date of acceptance of the application. The published contents of an application shall include the serial number and filing date of the application, the representative agent (if any), the registrant, the owner, the denomination of the plant variety, the name of the plant species and the date on which the application was accepted as valid.

VI. Substantive Examination

208. The State administrative body for rights to plant varieties shall conduct a substantive examination of applications already accepted as valid. The examination shall cover:

(a) examination of the novelty and proper denomination of the plant variety;
(b) examination of results of technical tests of the plant variety.

Technical tests mean experiments conducted to determine the distinctness, uniformity and stability of a plant variety. The technical tests are conducted by the competent State body or by a person capable of testing plant varieties in compliance with the regulations of the Ministry of Agriculture and Rural Development. The State administrative body for rights to plant varieties may use previously obtained technical test results.

The time limit for examination of technical test results is ninety days from the date of receipt of such technical test results.

209. Before the relevant State administrative body for rights to plant varieties notifies a refusal to grant a plant variety protection certificate or notifies its decision to grant a plant variety protection certificate, the registrant has the following rights:

(a) To amend or supplement the application without changing the nature of the application.
(b) To request the recording of changes in the registrant's name or address.
(c) To request the recording of a change of registrant due to assignment of the application pursuant to a contract or as a result of inheritance or bequest.

Likewise, before the relevant State administrative body for rights to plant varieties decides whether to grant a plant variety protection certificate, the registrant may withdraw the application.[45] A request for withdrawal of an application must be made in writing.

45. Article 180 IPL.

From the moment a registrant withdraws an application for registration for protection, all subsequent procedures related to such application shall cease, and fees and charges already paid for procedures which have not yet been carried out are refunded at the request of the registrant.

210. Where an application for registration for protection is not rejected and the registrant pays the fee, the State administrative body for rights to plant varieties shall issue a decision granting a plant variety protection certificate and shall record it in the National Register of Protected Plant Varieties.

The registrant and any third party have the right to lodge a complaint about the grant or refusal to grant a plant variety protection certificate in compliance with the law on complaints and denunciations.

VII. Opinions of Third Parties on the Grant of a Plant Variety Protection Certificate

211. From the date of publication of an application for registration for protection of a plant variety in a specialized magazine on plant varieties until a decision on grant of a plant variety protection certificate is issued, any third party is permitted to provide an opinion to the State administrative body for rights to plant varieties challenging the grant of the plant variety protection certificate. The opinion must be made in writing and accompanied by supporting documents and evidence.

VIII. Refusal to Grant a Plant Variety Protection Certificate

212. An application for registration for protection is rejected, and the grant of a plant variety protection certificate is refused where the relevant plant variety fails to satisfy the conditions stipulated in Articles 176 and 178 of IPL. When a plant variety protection certificate is refused, the State administrative body for rights to plant varieties shall carry out the following procedures:

(1) Notify the intended refusal to grant a plant variety protection certificate, clearly stating the reasons for refusal and setting a time limit for the registrant to correct errors or oppose the intended refusal.
(2) Notify the refusal to grant a plant variety protection certificate where the registrant has failed to correct errors and has not opposed the intended refusal stipulated in clause 1 above.
(3) Carry out the procedures stipulated in Article 183 of IPL where the registrant has corrected errors or made a justifiable opposition to the intended refusal stipulated in clause 1 above.

IX. Suspension and Restoration of Validity of Plant Variety Protection Certificates

213. The validity of a plant variety protection certificate may be suspended in the following cases:[46]

(a) The protected plant variety no longer satisfies the conditions of uniformity and stability established at the time of grant of the certificate.
(b) The protection certificate holder fails to pay the validity maintenance fee according to regulations.
(c) The protection certificate holder fails to supply necessary documents and reproductive materials for maintaining and preserving the plant variety according to regulations.
(d) The protection certificate holder fails to change the denomination of the plant variety at the request of the State administrative body for rights to plant varieties.

214. In the cases stipulated in sub-paragraphs (a), (c) and (d) above, the relevant State administrative body for rights to plant varieties shall issue a decision on suspension of validity of the plant variety protection certificate.

In the case stipulated in sub-paragraph (b) above, upon the expiry of the time-limit for payment of the validity maintenance fee, the relevant State administrative body for rights to plant varieties shall issue a decision on suspension of validity of the plant variety protection certificate effective from the first day of the next valid year for which the validity maintenance fee was not paid.

In the case stipulated in sub-paragraph (a) above, any person may request the State administrative body for rights to plant varieties to suspend the validity of the plant variety protection certificate. Based on consideration of the application for suspension of a plant variety protection certificate and the opinions of relevant parties, the relevant State administrative body for rights to plant varieties shall either issue a decision to suspend the validity of the certificate or refuse the application.

In the cases stipulated in clause 1 of this article, the relevant State administrative body for rights to plant varieties shall publish such suspension in a specialized magazine, clearly stating the reasons for suspension, and shall concurrently send a notice thereon to the certificate holder. Within thirty days from the date of notification, the certificate holder may file a request for permission to remedy the reasons why validity was suspended with the State administrative body for rights to plant varieties and pay the fee for restoration of validity of the plant variety protection certificate. Within ninety days after the date of filing the request, the protection certificate holder must remedy the reasons why validity was suspended, applicable to the cases stipulated in sub-paragraphs (b), (c) and (d) above. The State administrative body for rights to plant varieties shall consider and restore the validity of the protection certificate and publish such restoration in a specialized magazine.

46. Article 170 IPL.

In the case stipulated in sub-paragraph (a) above, the validity of the plant variety protection certificate is restored after its holder successfully proves that the plant variety has satisfied the conditions of uniformity and stability and after this has been certified by the State administrative body for rights to plant varieties.

X. Cancellation of Effectiveness of Plant Variety Protection Certificates

215. The effectiveness of a plant variety protection certificate is cancelled in the following cases:

(a) The application for registration for protection of the plant variety was filed in the name of a person who did not have the registration right, except where the right to such plant variety was assigned to the holder of the registration right.
(b) The protected plant variety failed to satisfy the conditions of novelty or distinctness at the time of grant of the plant variety protection certificate.
(c) The plant variety failed to satisfy the conditions of uniformity or stability where the plant variety protection certificate was granted on the basis of the results of technical tests conducted by the registrant.

216. During the valid term of a plant variety protection certificate, any person may request the State administrative body for rights to plant varieties to cancel the effectiveness of a plant variety protection certificate. Based on the results of the examination of a request for cancellation of the effectiveness of a plant variety protection certificate and the opinions of the relevant parties, the State administrative body for rights to plant varieties shall either issue a notice of refusal to cancel or shall issue a decision on cancellation of the effectiveness of the plant variety protection certificate.

Where a plant variety protection certificate is cancelled, all transactions arising on the basis of the grant of the plant variety protection certificate are null and void, and such null and void transactions are dealt with in compliance with the Civil Code.

§5. Ownership and Transfer (Assignment: Licences)

I. Ownership

217. Rightholders whose rights to plant varieties are eligible for protection means those who select and breed or discover and develop plant varieties, those who invest in the selection and breeding or the discovery and development of plant varieties, or those to whom rights to plant varieties are transferred. They may include Vietnamese rightholders, rightholders from foreign countries which have concluded agreements on the protection of plant varieties with the Socialist Republic of Vietnam, and foreign rightholders with permanent residential addresses in Vietnam or with establishments producing or trading in plant varieties in Vietnam.

218. As noted, in order to obtain protection of rights to plant varieties, a person must file an application for registration for protection with the State administrative body for rights to plant varieties. Rightholders having the right to register plant varieties for protection (hereinafter referred to as registrants) shall include:

(a) breeders who have personally selected and bred or discovered and developed the plant variety by their own efforts and at their own expense;
(b) rightholders who fund breeders to select and breed or discover and develop the plant variety by job assignment or hiring, unless otherwise agreed;
(c) rightholders to whom are transferred or who inherit the right to register for protection of the plant variety.

For plant varieties which are selected and bred or discovered and developed with the use of State Budget funds or under projects managed by the State, the rights to such plant varieties belong to the State. The Government shall issue specific regulations governing the registration of rights to plant varieties stipulated in this clause.

II. Licensing of Plant Varieties

219. Licensing of a plant variety means permission from the protection certificate holder granted to another person to conduct one or more acts within the holder's right to use the plant variety. Where the right to use a plant variety is under co-ownership, the licensing of such plant variety to another person must be agreed to by all co-owners. The licensing of a plant variety must be effected in the form of a written contract.

The licensor has the right to permit or not permit the licensee to sub-license to a third party. The licensee has the following rights:

(a) To license the right to use to a third party if so permitted by the licensor.
(b) To request the licensor to take necessary and appropriate measures to prevent infringement by a third party causing loss and damage to the licensee.
(c) To take necessary measures to prevent a third party's infringements if, within a time limit of three months from the date of receipt of the request stipulated in sub-paragraph (b) above, the licensor fails to act as requested.

A plant variety licensing contract must not contain terms which unreasonably restrict the rights of the licensee, particularly restrictions neither derived from nor aimed at protecting the rights of the licensor to the licensed plant variety.

III. Assignment of Rights to Plant Varieties

220. Assignment of rights to a plant variety means the transfer by the plant variety protection certificate holder to the assignee of all rights to such plant variety. The assignee becomes the plant variety protection certificate holder from the date of registration of the assignment contract with the State administrative body for rights to plant varieties in accordance with procedures stipulated by law. Where rights to a plant variety are under joint ownership, all co-owners must consent to the assignment of rights to another person. The assignment of rights to a plant variety must be effected in the form of written contract.

§6. Scope of Exclusive Rights

I. Rights of Breeders of Plant Varieties

221. The breeder of a plant variety has the following rights:[47]

(1) To have his or her name recorded as the breeder in the plant variety protection certificate, the National Register of Protected Plant Varieties, and published documents on the plant variety.
(2) To receive remuneration pursuant to the provisions of clause 1(a) of Article 191 of IPL.

222. A protection certificate holder has the right to exercise or authorize others to exercise the following rights to reproductive materials of a protected plant variety:

(a) To conduct production or propagation.
(b) To process the reproductive materials for the purpose of propagation.
(c) To offer the reproductive materials for sale.
(d) To sell the reproductive materials or to conduct other marketing activities.
(e) To export the reproductive materials.
(f) To import the reproductive materials.
(g) To stock reproductive materials for the purposes specified in sub-paragraphs (a) to (f) inclusive above.

A protection certificate holder also has the right to prevent others from using the plant variety to bequeath or transfer the rights to the plant variety.

II. Extension of Rights of Protection Certificate Holders

223. The rights of a protection certificate holder are extended to the following plant varieties:[48]

(1) Plant varieties which originate from the protected plant variety, except where such protected plant variety itself originates from another protected plant variety.

47. Article 185 IPL.
48. Article 187 IPL.

(2) A plant variety is deemed to originate from a protected plant variety if such plant variety still retains the expression of the essential characteristics resulting from the genotype or combination of genotypes of the protected variety, except for differences resulting from an impact on the protected variety.
(3) Plant varieties which are not definitely distinct from the protected plant variety.
(4) Plant varieties, the production of which requires the repeated use of the protected plant variety.

III. Obligations of Protection Certificate Holders and Breeders of Plant Varieties

224. A protection certificate holder has the following obligations:

(a) To pay remuneration to the breeder of the plant variety as agreed upon; in the absence of such agreement, the remuneration level must comply with the provisions of law.
(b) To pay the fee for maintenance of validity of the plant variety protection certificate in accordance with regulations.
(c) To preserve the protected plant variety, to supply information and reproductive materials of the protected plant variety upon request of the State administrative body for plant varieties protection, and to maintain the stability of the protected plant variety in accordance with characteristics described at the time of granting the Plant Variety Protection Certificate.

§7. Limitations of the Scope of Protection: Compulsory Licences

I. Limitations on Rights of Plant Variety Protection Certificate Holders

225. The following acts shall not be deemed an infringement of the right to a protected plant variety:

(a) Using the plant variety for personal and non-commercial purposes.
(b) Using the plant variety for cross-breeding for scientific research purposes.
(c) Using the plant variety to create new plant varieties distinct from the protected plant varieties.
(d) Using harvested materials of the protected plant variety by an individual production household for self-propagation and cultivation in the next season on the land area belonging to such household.

226. The right to a plant variety shall not be applicable to acts related to materials of the protected plant variety which are sold on or otherwise brought onto the domestic or overseas market by the protection certificate holder or his or her licensee, except for the following acts:

(a) acts relating to further propagation of such plant variety; and
(b) acts relating to the export of reproductive materials of such plant variety to countries where the genus or species of such plant variety is not protected, except where such materials are exported for consumption purposes.

II. Compulsory Licensing of Plant Varieties

A. *Conditions of Compulsory Licensing*

227. In the following cases, the rights to use a plant variety may be licensed to another person pursuant to a decision of the competent State body without permission from the protection certificate holder or his or her exclusive licensee (hereinafter referred to as the holder of the exclusive right to use the plant variety):

(a) The use of such plant variety is for the public interest and non-commercial purposes, in the service of national defence and security, for the food security and nutrition of the people, or to meet other urgent social needs.
(b) The persons having the need and capacity to use such plant variety fail to reach an agreement with the holder of the exclusive right to use such plant variety on the entry into a licensing contract, though they have made their best efforts within a reasonable period of time to negotiate satisfactory price and commercial conditions.
(c) The holder of the exclusive right to use such plant variety is deemed to have conducted anti-competitive practices prohibited by the law on competition.

228. The holder of the exclusive right to use a plant variety may request termination of the use right when the bases for licensing stipulated in clause 1 of this article cease to exist and are unlikely to recur, provided that termination of such use right will not be prejudicial to the licensee.

The right to use a plant variety licensed pursuant to a decision of a competent State body must satisfy the following conditions:

(a) Such licensed use right is non-exclusive.
(b) Such licensed use right is limited to a scope and duration sufficient to attain the licensing objective and is largely for the domestic market, except for the case stipulated in sub-paragraph (c).
(c) The licensee must not assign the use right to another person, except where the assignment is made together with the transfer of the business establishment of the licensee, and the licensee must not sub-license to others.
(d) The licensee must pay adequate compensation to the holder of the exclusive right to use the plant variety, taking into account the economic value of such use right in each specific case and in compliance with the compensation rate bracket promulgated by the Government. The Government shall specify cases of compulsory licensing of plant varieties and the compensation rate bracket.

229. The Ministry of Agriculture and Rural Development shall issue decisions on the licensing of plant varieties in the domains over which such Ministry exercises State management on the basis of considering licensing requests for the cases stipulated above. Likewise, ministries and ministerial equivalent bodies shall, after consulting the opinion of the Ministry of Agriculture and Rural Development, issue decisions on the licensing of plant varieties in domains under their respective management.

Plant variety licensing decisions must set the scope of use and any conditions. The State body competent to issue a decision licensing a plant variety must promptly notify the holder of the exclusive right to use the plant variety in question of such decision. In addition, decisions on the licensing of plant varieties or refusal to license plant varieties may be subject to complaints or lawsuits.

B. *Rights of Protection Certificate Holders in Cases of Compulsory Licensing of Plant Varieties*

230. Under Article 197 IPL, a protection certificate holder subject to compulsorily licensing of the plant variety has the following rights:

(1) To receive compensation corresponding to the economic value of the licensed use right or equivalent to the licensing price under a contract with an equivalent scope and term.
(2) To request the State administrative body for rights to plant varieties to amend, terminate the validity of or invalidate the compulsory licensing when the conditions for such compulsory licensing no longer exist and when such amendment, termination of validity or invalidation will not cause loss and damage to the licensees who derived their right from the compulsory licensing.

§8. Duration of Protection

231. A plant variety protection certificate is valid throughout the entire territory of Vietnam. Plant variety protection certificates are valid from the grant date until the expiry of a period of twenty-five years for timber trees and vines and twenty years for other plant varieties, except when their validity is terminated, or they are invalidated.

§9. Infringement and Remedies

232. The regulations on infringement and remedies for plant variety are similar to those of other industrial properties, except for the following details.

I. Acts Constituting an Infringement of the Right to a Plant Variety

233. The following acts are deemed an infringement of the rights of a protection certificate holder:

(1) Exploiting or using the rights of such protection certificate holder without his or her permission.
(2) Using a plant variety denomination which is identical or similar to a denomination protected for a plant variety of the same species or a species closely linked to the protected plant variety.
(3) Using a protected plant variety without paying remuneration.

II. Provisional Rights to Plant Varieties

234. Provisional rights to a plant variety are the rights of the registrant for protection of such plant variety which arise from the date of publication of the application for registration for protection until the date of grant of the plant variety protection certificate. Where a plant variety protection certificate is not granted for such plant variety, the protection registrant shall no longer have these provisional rights.

235. Where the registrant is aware of the fact that another person has exercised the owner's rights stipulated in Articles 186 and 187 of the IPL, from the moment the application is duly accepted, the plant variety protection registrant may notify in writing this user of the fact that an application for registration for protection of the plant variety has been filed, clearly specifying the filing date and the date of duly acceptance of such application, so that the user may either stop using or continue using the plant variety.

Where a user who has been notified continues using the plant variety, the plant variety protection certificate holder has the right, upon the grant of the certificate, to demand such plant variety user pay compensation equivalent to the licensing price of such plant variety within the corresponding scope of use and duration.

§10. Overlapping and Relation to Other Intellectual Property Laws

236. Although there could be an overlap between plant variety rights and patent rights for biotechnology processes, there has not been any precedent in Vietnam presenting such a situation. The laws and regulations are also silent as to how to deal with such overlap.

Chapter 8. Chip Protection

§1. Sources: Legislation

237. Chip protection (or layout design protection) is regulated in Chapter III (industrial property rights) of IPL. It was newly introduced in the Vietnam legal system in 2004 following the Vietnam-US Bilateral Trade Agreement. This protection regime relates to the design of semi-conducting closed circuits (hereinafter referred to as layout design). Layout design means a three-dimensional disposition of circuit elements and their interconnections in a semi-conducting closed circuit. Semiconductor integrated circuit means a product in its intermediate or final form in which the elements (at least one of which is an active element) and some or all of the interconnections are integrally formed in or on a piece of semiconductor material. Further, the product must be intended to perform an electronic function. Integrated circuit is synonymous with IC, chip and micro-electronic circuit.[49] So far, no layout designs have been registered at the NOIP, and the practical purpose of this regime is also not clear.

§2. Subject Matter of Protection

238. A layout design is eligible for protection when if it is both original and commercially novel.

Principles, processes, systems and methods operated by semiconductor integrated circuits and information or software contained in semiconductor integrated circuits are ineligible for protection as layout designs.

§3. Conditions of Protection

I. Originality of Layout Designs

239. A layout design is deemed to be original if it satisfies the following conditions:

(a) It is the result of its author's creative labour.
(b) It was not widely known among creators of layout designs or manufacturers of semi-conducting closed circuits at the time of its creation.

A layout design which is a combination of elements and common interconnections is deemed to be original only if such combination, taken overall, is original pursuant to the provisions of clause 1 of this article.

49. Articles 4.14 and 4.15 IPL.

II. Commercial Novelty of Layout Designs

240. A layout design is deemed to be commercially novel if it has not yet been commercially exploited anywhere in the world prior to the filing date of the application for registration.

A layout design shall not be deemed to have lost its commercial novelty if the application for registration of the layout design is filed within two years from the date the layout design was commercially exploited for the first time anywhere in the world by the person who has the right to register it as defined in Article 86 of IPL or by his or her licensee.

241. Commercial exploitation of a layout design as stipulated in clause 2 of this article means any act of public distribution for commercial purposes of a semiconductor integrated circuit produced by incorporation of such layout design or of a commodity containing such semiconductor integrated circuit.

§4. Formalities (Procedure for Grant and Obtaining Protection)

242. The formalities for registration of layout design are similar to those for patents, except for some details. Under Article 104 IPL, documents, samples and information identifying a layout design which needs to be registered for protection in an application for registration of a layout design shall include:

(1) drawings and photos of the layout design;
(2) information on the functions and structure of semi-conducting closed circuits produced under the layout design;
(3) samples of semi-conducting closed circuits produced under the layout design, if such layout design has been commercially exploited;
(4) applications for registration of layout designs shall not be substantively examined.

243. Applications for registration of layout designs are published by means of permitting direct access at NOIP for industrial property rights, provided that reproduction shall not be permitted. Access to confidential information in an application shall only be permitted to competent authorities and parties involved in the process of carrying out procedures for invalidating protection titles or the process of carrying out procedures for dealing with infringement of rights. Principal information on an application for registration of a layout design and the protection title for a layout design is published within two months from the date of grant of such protection title.

§5. Ownership and Transfer (Assignment: Licences)

244. The right to register layout designs shall belong to authors who have created inventions by their own labour and at their own expense, or people who have supplied funds and material facilities to authors in the form of job assignment or hiring, unless otherwise agreed by the parties involved. A person who has the registration right as stipulated in this article may assign such right to other persons by a written contract, bequest or inheritance, even where a registration application has already been filed.

If the layout designs are created by using material, technical facilities and funds from the State Budget, then the State shall have the right to register such layout designs and may be allowed to become the co-owner of the layout designs if they are created partly from the State Budget. Where a number of rightholders have jointly created or invested in the creation of a layout design, such rightholders shall all have the registration right which may only be exercised with the consensus of all.

245. The eligible applicants, once granted the layout designs, shall become the layout design owners. However, the law also provides protection to the authors, that is, those who have personally created the patent. Where two or more persons have jointly created an industrial property object, they are co-authors of it. These authors shall enjoy moral rights, namely the right to be named as authors in the patents or utility model patents and to be acknowledged as authors in documents in which inventions are published or introduced. Moreover, authors shall also enjoy economic rights to receive remuneration.

246. Layout design assignment is similar to that for patents (*see* paragraph 92 above). A layout design assignment contract is valid upon its registration with NOIP. Regulations on the order and procedures for receiving and processing application files for registration of layout designs licence contracts and of industrial property right assignment contracts are provided in Decree No. 65/2023/ND-CP dated 23 August 2023, detailing and guiding the implementation of the IPL regarding industrial property, protection of industrial property rights, rights to plant varieties, and state management of intellectual property.

§6. Scope of Exclusive Rights

247. As with patents, the design owner has the exclusive right to use the design, to dispose of the design and to prevent others from using the design without his consent (except when limited use is allowed). Use of a layout design means the performance of the following acts:

(a) Reproducing the layout design; manufacturing semi-conducting closed circuits under the protected layout design.
(b) Selling, leasing, advertising, offering or stocking copies of the protected layout design, semi-conducting closed circuits manufactured under the protected layout design or articles containing such semi-conducting closed circuits.
(c) Importing copies of the protected layout design, semi-conducting closed circuits manufactured under the protected layout design or articles containing such semi-conducting closed circuits.

248. Provisional rights (which are similar to patent provisional rights) are defined as the circumstance where a layout design has, before the grant date of the certificate of registered design of semi-conducting closed circuits, been commercially exploited by the person with the registration right or his or her licensee. If such a person knows that such layout design is being used by another person for commercial purposes, then he or she may notify in writing the user of his or her registration right so that the user may either terminate or continue such use.

§7. Limitations of the Scope of Protection

249. The limitations of the scope of protection for layout design are similar to those for patents (*see* Chapter 2 §5 II above). In addition, use of a layout design without knowing or having the obligation to know that such layout design is under protection is also allowed without the permission of the layout design owner.

§8. Duration of Protection

250. A certificate of registered design of semi-conducting closed circuits is valid from the grant date until the earliest of the following dates:

(a) The end of ten years after the filing date.
(b) The end of ten years after the date the layout design was first commercially exploited anywhere in the world by a person with the registration right or his or her licensee.
(c) The end of fifteen years after the date of creation of the layout design.

§9. Infringement and Remedies

251. The regulations on infringement and remedies for layout design are similar to those of other industrial properties, particularly patents and trademarks (*see* Chapter 2 §9 and Chapter 4 §10 above).

§10. Overlapping and Relation to Other Intellectual Property Laws

252. There can be an overlap between the protection of copyright and layout design. However, each of the rights protects a different aspect of creativity. If there is an overlap between layout design and copyright, the right over the layout design usually prevails because layout design is an exclusive right to use a design and prevent others from using that design (regardless of whether the use was a copy or not), whereas copyright is only a right to prevent the copying of a work.

Chapter 9. Trade Secrets/Confidential Information

§1. Sources: Legislation

253. Trade secret means information obtained from activities of financial or intellectual investment which has not yet been disclosed and which can be used in business.[50] Compared to patents, trade secrets entered the scope of protection later (not until Decree No. 54/2000/ND-CP, as a result of Vietnam entering into the Vietnam US Bilateral Trade Agreement). Trade secret protection is provided in Chapter III of IPL, in the same section as patent protection. Industrial property rights to a trade secret are established on the basis of lawful use thereof. It is not required to register trade secrets at NOIP in order for them to be protected, and this is generally considered a backup solution when a claim for patent infringement is not successful, either because the scope of patent protection does not reach the item, or because the technology is not yet registered for patent protection at NOIP. Industrial property rights to a trade secret are established on the basis of lawful acquirement of the trade secret and maintaining its confidentiality.

§2. The Protection of Trade Secrets/Confidential Information

254. A trade secret is eligible for protection when it satisfies the following conditions:[51]

(1) It is neither common knowledge nor easily obtainable.
(2) When used in business activities, the trade secret will create advantages for its holder over those who do not hold or use it.
(3) The owner of the trade secret maintains its secrecy by necessary means so that the secret will not be disclosed nor be easily accessible.

255. The following confidential information is ineligible for protection as trade secrets and will be subject to a different regime of protection:

(1) Personal identification secrets.
(2) State management secrets.
(3) National defence and security secrets.
(4) Other confidential information unrelated to business.

§3. Ownership, Scope of Protection and Transfer

256. Owner of a trade secret means a person who has lawfully acquired such trade secret and kept it secret. A trade secret acquired by an employee or a performer of an

50. Article 4.23 IPL.
51. Article 84 IPL.

assigned task during the performance of the hired job or assigned task is owned by the employer or the task assignor unless otherwise agreed by the parties.

Once the owner of a trade secret, the owner has the right to prohibit others from disclosing or using such secret. Use of a trade secret means the performance of the following acts:

(a) Applying the trade secret to the manufacture of products, provision of services or trade in goods.
(b) Selling, advertising for sale, stocking for sale or importing products manufactured with the application of the trade secret.

257. Under Article 127 IPL, the following acts are deemed infringements of the right to trade secrets:

(a) Accessing or acquiring information pertaining to a trade secret by taking acts against secrecy-keeping measures applied by lawful controllers of such trade secret.
(b) Disclosing or using information pertaining to a trade secret without the permission of the owner of such trade secret.
(c) Breaching secrecy-keeping contracts or deceiving, inducing, buying off, forcing, seducing or abusing the trust of persons in charge of secrecy-keeping in order to access, acquire or disclose a trade secret.
(d) Accessing or acquiring information pertaining to the trade secret of an applicant for a licence for trading in or circulating products by taking acts against secrecy-keeping measures applied by competent bodies.
(e) Using or disclosing trade secrets while knowing or having the obligation to know that they have been acquired by others engaged in one of the acts stipulated in sub-paragraphs (a), (b), (c) or (d) above.
(f) Failing to perform the secrecy-keeping obligation stipulated in Article 128 of IPL.

Lawful controllers of trade secrets defined above include owners of trade secrets, their lawful licensees and managers of trade secrets.

258. Please note that owners of trade secrets shall not have the right to prevent others from performing the following acts:

(a) Disclosing or using trade secrets acquired without knowing or having the obligation to know that they were unlawfully acquired by others.
(b) Disclosing secret data in order to protect the public according to the provisions of clause 1 of Article 128 of IPL.
(c) Using secret data stipulated in Article 128 of IPL, not for commercial purposes.
(d) Disclosing or using trade secrets obtained independently.
(e) Disclosing or using trade secrets obtained by analysing or evaluating lawfully distributed products unless otherwise agreed upon by analysers or evaluators and owners of such trade secrets or sellers of such products.

§4. Obligation to Protect Test Data

259. Article 128 IPL provides that where the law requires applicants for licences for circulating pharmaceuticals or agro-chemical products to supply test results or any other trade secret data obtained by investment of considerable effort, and where applicants request such data to be kept secret, the competent licensing body must apply necessary measures so that such data is neither used for unfair commercial purposes nor disclosed, except where the disclosure is necessary to protect the public.

260. For pharmaceuticals, from the time of submission of secret data in applications to the competent body to the end of a five-year term from the date the applicant is granted a licence, such body must not grant licences to any subsequent applicants whose applications use the said secret data without the consent of submitters of such data, except when the applications use trade secrets obtained independently.

261. In the case where the competent authority for drug circulation permits the applicant based on the fact that a drug has been licensed for circulation or data demonstrating the safety and efficacy of a drug that has been licensed for circulation to apply for a circulation licence for another drug, the competent licensing authority must disclose on its Electronic Information Portal or Electronic Information Page the information of the subsequent applicant within a period of five months before the drug in the subsequent application is licensed for circulation, unless the issuance of the circulation licence needs to be done earlier as stipulated by other relevant laws.

262. For agricultural chemicals, from the date the confidential data in the licence application is submitted to the competent authority until the expiration of ten years from the date the applicant is licensed, the authority shall not license the late applicant based on the use of the confidential data mentioned above or based on the fact that the entity submitting the confidential data has been licensed for circulation without the consent of the data submitter, except in cases of disclosure, use of independently generated business confidential information, or when licensing is necessary to ensure national defence, security, nutrition for the people, or meet other essential societal needs.

Chapter 10. Geographical Indications and Appellations of Origin

§1. SOURCES: LEGISLATION

263. Geographical indication means the sign used to identify a product as originating from a specific region, locality, territory or country.[52] Until Decree No. 54/2000/ND-CP, geographical indications are known as appellations of origin. Nowadays, geographical indications are provided in Chapter III of IPL and are required to be registered at NOIP to be protected.

§2. SUBJECT MATTERS OF PROTECTION

264. A geographical indication is eligible for protection when it satisfies the following conditions:

(1) The product bearing the geographical indication originates from the area, locality, territory or country corresponding to such geographical indication.
(2) The product bearing the geographical indication has a reputation, quality or characteristics mainly attributable to geographical conditions of the area, locality, territory or country corresponding to such geographical indication.

265. Geographical areas bearing geographical indications must have their boundaries accurately determined by words and maps.

The following objects are ineligible for protection as geographical indications:

(1) Names or indications which have become generic names of goods in Vietnam.
(2) Geographical indications of foreign countries where they are not, or are no longer, protected or used.
(3) Geographical indications identical with or similar to a protected mark, where the use of such geographical indication is likely to cause confusion as to the origin of products.
(4) Geographical indications which mislead consumers as to the true geographical origin of products bearing such geographical indications.

§3. CONDITIONS OF PROTECTION

266. To be protected, a geographical indication must be associated with reputation, quality and characteristics of products bearing such geographical indication. Reputation of products bearing a geographical indication is determined on the basis of the trust of consumers in such products, to the extent such products are widely

52. Article 4.22 IPL.

known to and selected by consumers. Quality and characteristics of products bearing a geographical indication are determined by one or more qualitative, quantitative, physically, chemically, or microbiologically perceptible criteria which can be tested by technical means or by experts with appropriate testing methods. The factors relevant to the quality, reputation and characteristics of products are the following:

(a) Geographical conditions relevant to a geographical indication means natural and human factors which are decisive to the reputation, quality and characteristics of products bearing such geographical indication.[53]
(b) Natural factors shall include climatic, hydrological, geological, topographical and ecological factors and other natural conditions.
(c) Human factors shall include the skills and expertise of producers and traditional production processes of localities.

§4. Formalities of Protection

267. Under Article 106 IPL, to be protected, the applicant must apply for registration of geographical indications. The documents, samples and information identifying a geographical indication which needs to be registered for protection in an application for registration of a geographical indication shall include:

(a) the name or sign being the geographical indication;
(b) the product bearing the geographical indication;
(c) description of peculiar characteristics and quality or reputation of the product bearing the geographical indication and particular elements of natural conditions decisive to the peculiar characteristics and quality or reputation of the product (hereinafter referred to as the description of peculiar characteristics);
(d) map of the geographical area bearing the geographical indication;
(e) documents providing evidence that the geographical indication is under protection in the country of origin in the case of a foreign geographical origin;
(f) for homonymous geographical indications, documents explaining the conditions of use and how to present geographical indications to ensure the ability to distinguish between geographical indications.

268. The description of peculiar characteristics must contain the following principal contents:

(a) Description of the relevant product, including raw materials and physical, chemical, microbiological and other perceptible properties of the product.
(b) Method of identification of the geographical area bearing the geographical indication.
(c) Evidence proving that the product originates from such a geographical area.

53. Article 82 IPL.

(d) Description of local and stable methods of production and processing.
(e) Information on the relationship between the peculiar characteristics and quality or reputation of the product and the geographical conditions.
(f) Information on the mechanism of self-control of the peculiar characteristics or quality of the product.

Once protected, a protection title of a geographical indication shall record the organization managing such geographical indication, the person having the right to use such geographical indication, the protected geographical indication, the particular characteristics of products bearing such geographical indication, and the particular characteristics of geographical conditions and geographical areas bearing such geographical indication.

A certificate of registered geographical indication has indefinite validity starting from the grant date.

269. Rightholders who are granted by the State the right to use or the right to manage geographical indications have the following rights:

(a) Organizations which are granted the right to manage geographical indications may permit other persons to use such geographical indications.
(b) Rightholders who are granted the right to use or organizations which are granted the right to manage geographical indications may prevent other persons from using such geographical indications.

Use of a geographical indication means the performance of the following acts:[54]

(a) Affixing the protected geographical indication in or on goods or goods packages, business facilities, and transaction documents in business activities.
(b) Circulating, offering, advertising for sale or stocking for sale goods bearing the protected geographical indication.
(c) Importing goods bearing the protected geographical indication.

§5. Ownership, Early Termination and Transfer

270. The right to register Vietnamese geographical indications belongs to the State. The State shall permit rightholders producing products bearing geographical indications, collective organizations representing such persons, and administrative bodies of localities to which such geographical indications pertain, to exercise the right to register geographical indications. Persons who exercise the right to register geographical indications shall not become owners of such geographical indications.

54. Clause 4 of Art. 121 IPL.

271. As for foreign geographical indications, the right to register belongs to the owner of such foreign geographical indications in the country of origin (where the territory of such indications is located).

As noted, the State is the owner of geographical indications of Vietnam. The State shall grant the right to use geographical indications to persons who manufacture products bearing such geographical indications in relevant localities and put such products on the market. The State shall directly exercise the right to manage geographical indications or grant that right to organizations representing the interests of all persons granted the right to use geographical indications.

272. The geographical indications registration certificate may be terminated by NOIP if the geographical conditions decisive to the reputation, quality or special characteristics of products bearing a geographical indication have changed, resulting in the loss of such reputation, quality or characteristics of products.

Rights to geographical indications shall not be assignable and shall not be licensable.

§6. Infringements and Remedies

273. The following acts are deemed to be infringements of the right to protected geographical indications:

(a) Using protected geographical indications for products which do not satisfy the criteria of peculiar characteristics and quality of products bearing geographical indications, although such products originate from geographical areas bearing such geographical indication.
(b) Using protected geographical indications for products similar to products bearing geographical indications for the purpose of taking advantage of their reputation and popularity.
(c) Using any sign identical with, or similar to, a protected geographical indication for products not originating from geographical areas bearing such geographical indication, and therefore misleading consumers into believing such products originate from such geographical areas.
(d) Using protected geographical indications of wines or spirits for wines or spirits not originating from geographical areas bearing such geographical indication, even where the true origin of goods is indicated, or geographical indications are used in the form of translations or transcriptions, or accompanied by such words as ‘category’, ‘model’, ‘type’, ‘imitation’ or the like.

Selected Bibliography

Japan Patent Office. *Standard Textbook on Patent*. 2001 (in Vietnamese).

Hanoi Law University. *Teaching Intellectual Property Rights*. People's Police Press, 2006.

Le Net. *Intellectual Property Rights*. Ho Chi Minh City National University Press, 2006. 2nd edn. 2007.

Le Net. *Law and Economics*. Intellectual Press, 2007.

Le Net. *Patent Management in Vietnam*. Ho Chi Minh City Law University Press, 2010.

National Office of Intellectual Properties. *Basic Principles on Intellectual Property Rights*. WIPO Documents, 2008. National Office of Intellectual Properties. *Guidance on Patent Registration*. 2008.

Selected Bibliography

Index

The numbers here refer to paragraph numbers.

Advocate, 15
Agreement, 26, 57, 65, 71, 93, 98, 104, 105, 144, 148, 150, 166, 189, 199, 200, 217, 224, 227, 237, 253
Arbitration, 111
Assignment, 40–41, 90, 92–93, 95–96, 105, 141, 145–150, 181–182, 209, 217–220, 228, 244–246
Author, 26, 32–41, 44, 45, 50–53, 62, 88, 90, 91, 106, 181, 182, 239, 244, 245

Certificate, 24, 25, 33, 35, 80, 109, 133–136, 142, 143, 148, 154, 165, 187, 196, 199, 201–202, 209–216, 219–227, 230–231, 233–235, 248, 250, 268, 272
Co-author, 34, 38, 91, 182, 245
Compensation, 17, 97, 100, 105, 111, 121, 125, 126, 161, 228, 230, 235
Contract, 7, 12, 17, 25, 37, 39–42, 84, 89, 90, 92–95, 103, 104, 119, 122, 131, 147, 148, 150, 181, 209, 219, 220, 227, 230, 244, 246, 257
- civil, 17
- economic, 17
- enforcement, 12
- patent assignment, 92, 93, 246

Copyright, 20–64, 129, 142, 165, 187, 252
- holder, 26, 33–35, 37, 39–41, 45–48, 50–52, 57–59, 64, 165

Criminalization of civil cases, 17

Declaration, 34, 73, 75, 76, 93, 107, 143, 203
Dispute, 6, 13, 17, 33, 64, 131

Geographical indication, 21–22, 24, 75, 88, 89, 134, 135, 142, 144, 152, 156, 157, 167, 169, 170, 180, 195, 263–273
Geographical origin of goods, 142, 146, 152
Grant, 33, 35, 41, 45, 65, 66, 71–89, 94, 104–107, 116, 136–138, 143, 148, 154, 178–180, 185, 189, 197–216, 231, 234, 235, 242, 243, 248, 250, 260, 268, 271

Identity, 9
Industrial design, 20, 22, 24, 64, 72, 75, 81, 89, 90, 97–101, 129, 134, 142, 144, 158, 165, 171–187
Industrial property, 19–22, 25, 65, 75, 76, 79–81, 84–89, 91, 93, 95, 97, 99, 101, 107, 119, 121–123, 125, 127, 130–136, 143, 160, 166, 171, 182, 237, 243, 245, 246, 253
- object, 80, 91, 95, 119, 122, 182, 245
- representation services, 130–136

Infringement, 62–63, 65, 100, 111–128, 139, 155–164, 166, 168, 186, 219, 225, 232–235, 243, 251, 253, 257, 273
Inheritance, 37, 84, 90, 147, 181, 205, 209, 244
Intellectual property, 3, 19–23, 25, 64–65, 93, 112–124, 127–130, 156–165, 187, 236, 246, 252
- rightholders, 112, 117–118, 121, 128, 158

Interpretation, 11, 18
Invalidation, 74, 110, 142, 230
IPL, 19–27, 30, 32–34, 36–41, 43, 45, 50–53, 61–66, 75, 81, 85, 89, 93, 95, 98, 99, 102, 106, 108, 109, 115, 120, 129, 139, 142, 152, 153, 155, 156, 158–160, 165–168, 176, 187, 189, 197, 198, 212, 221, 230, 235–237, 240, 242, 246, 252, 253, 257–259, 263, 267

Index

Judge, 9, 13–14, 16, 18
Judiciary, 9, 13

Layout designs, 22, 24, 75, 89, 90, 97–99, 101, 129, 134, 237–252
Legal instrument, 24, 29
Legislation, 4, 11–12, 21

Mark, 22, 64, 72, 75, 140–157, 167, 169, 170
Mark owner, 88, 140, 144, 148, 150–152, 155, 156, 169
Modification, 9, 28

NOC, 23, 33, 35, 64
NOIP, 3, 19, 23, 75–76, 80–82, 84–89, 93, 95, 107, 110, 130, 135, 136, 143, 144, 166, 189, 237, 243, 246, 253, 263, 272

Obligation, 6, 9, 17, 40, 42, 62, 63, 92, 94, 96–99, 104, 118, 125, 130–132, 160, 161, 224, 249, 257–262
Ownership, 4, 25, 37–41, 57–59, 90–95, 124, 145–150, 153, 181–182, 217–220, 244–246, 256–258, 270–272

Patent, 65–68, 71–89, 91–101, 104, 106–111, 116, 119, 129–139, 143, 152, 156, 159, 178, 183, 185, 236, 245, 248, 253
  application, 67–68, 71–72, 82–83, 109
  assignment, 92, 93, 95
  license contract, 94–95
  owner, 91, 94–99, 101, 111, 116
  protection, 66, 71–89, 99–110, 152, 253
  registration, 24, 65, 73, 77, 81, 83, 108, 139
PCT, 65, 76, 85
Plaintiff, 15, 113, 119–122
Power of attorney, 15, 73–74, 93, 203–204
Prejudice, 38–40, 51–52, 60–61
Prior use, 96, 97, 99, 100, 101, 152
Procedure, 16–17, 25, 71–89, 93, 101, 114, 132, 139, 143–144, 157–164, 178–180, 189, 197–216, 220, 242–243, 246
Proof, 2, 33, 119, 168
Property, 3, 8–9, 19–23, 25, 62, 64–65, 75, 76, 79–81, 84–89, 91, 93, 95, 97, 99, 101, 107, 112–125, 127–136, 143, 156–166, 171, 182, 187, 236, 237, 243, 245, 246, 252, 253

Registration, 21–22, 24, 25, 33–35, 65, 67, 69, 73, 75, 77, 79–85, 87–90, 93, 95, 97, 100, 104, 108–110, 134, 139, 142–145, 147, 148, 152, 154, 165, 166, 172, 174–176, 178–182, 187, 189, 191, 192, 195, 197–200, 203–207, 209–212, 215, 218, 220, 234, 235, 240, 242–244, 246, 248, 250, 267, 272
  certificate, 24, 33, 142, 148, 272
  of a patent, 75, 82, 84, 93, 97, 100
  of industrial property, 21, 75, 79, 81, 84, 85, 87–89, 180
Remuneration, 45, 47, 49–52, 57, 60, 61, 91, 98, 99, 182, 221, 224, 233, 245
Right, 37–41, 44–50, 53, 57–59, 68, 72–73, 76, 79, 81, 89, 90, 92–97, 99–101, 103–106, 109–113, 116, 118–120, 122, 123, 125, 127, 145–149, 151–153, 158–160, 162, 165, 169, 175, 181–183, 187, 191, 200, 203, 205, 206, 210, 215, 218, 219, 222, 225–230, 233, 240, 244–248, 250, 252, 256–258, 268–271, 273
  adaptation, 48
  economic, 8, 37, 43–45, 50, 53, 57, 91, 182, 245
  exclusive, 43–50, 57–59, 94–96, 103–106, 151, 165, 183, 187, 221–224, 227–229, 247–248, 252
  exploitation, 45, 118, 128
  industrial property, 20–22, 25, 65, 75, 76, 88, 89, 93, 95, 99, 107, 121–123, 125, 127, 131, 132, 134, 143, 160, 166, 171, 237, 243, 246, 253
  intellectual property, 3, 20–23, 25, 64, 112–124, 127, 128, 157–164
  moral, 37, 39–41, 43, 44, 46, 50, 53, 57, 62, 91, 182, 245
  neighbouring, 41, 54–61
  of performers, 57, 60, 61, 63
  performing, 47
  public lending, 50
  publication, 44, 46, 53
  related, 24–25, 33, 35, 54–56, 60–63
  reproduction, 46
Right holder, 33, 35, 57–59, 100, 116–119, 122, 123, 127, 152, 159–164, 191

Socio-economic situation, 9
  sub-license contract, 94
  substantive examination period, 84

Technical specification, 78
Termination, 40, 42, 74, 83, 89, 95, 104, 107, 118, 127, 154, 228, 230, 270–272
Trademark: 19–20, 24, 36, 64, 129, 134, 135, 139, 140, 142–144, 148–152, 154–158, 161, 165, 166, 172, 186, 187, 251
  holder, 64
  owner, 148, 150–152
  protection, 139, 152
TRIPS, 23, 26, 30, 65, 66, 120

WIPO, 19, 26, 85

Index

www.ingramcontent.com/pod-product-compliance
Lightning Source LLC
Chambersburg PA
CBHW071351230926
51846CB00002B/505
* 9 7 8 9 4 0 3 5 1 4 5 8 1 *